New Earth Reiki

A Complete Guide for
Beginning to Advanced Healing Practitioners
For after the Shift

gia combs-ramirez, MA, RM

Soluna Press

Soluna Press
P.O. Box 1158
Ennis, MT 59729

Artwork by Robin Reints

In great appreciation, I dedicate this book to my sister, Deborah,
who asked for the chapter on Energy Anatomy
and continues to help beyond the veil to find
healing solutions for Multiple Sclerosis

Contents

Preface to the New Edition

"One moment you are walking down a road headed in a certain direction, happy or unhappy with your pace or destination, and in the next, some invisible force picks you up and sets you down on a completely different road with a different destination. Or so it seems at the time."
-gia combs-ramirez

"Why now, after 14 years of studying and promoting Crystalline Consciousness Technique™ are you publishing a book on Reiki?" my friend asked me. My short answer was it's like making a prequel to a story instead of a sequel. The longer answer is a bit more complicated.

In 1989, I studied massage therapy at the New Mexico Academy of Healing Arts. The extensive training had a foundation in Swedish massage with other modalities that were offered in an introductory format to acquaint us with different techniques. I was drawn to the energy modalities such as Polarity and Orthobionomy. After graduating, I continued to study Cranio Sacral Therapies with the Upledger Foundation, including SomatoEmotional Release and Trauma Release Therapy and then EMF Balancing with Peggy Phoenix Dubro.

What fascinated me with bodywork was getting to the root cause, not just treat symptoms. And I always wanted to get the biggest result for the least amount of effort. With those two motivating factors, I naturally veered toward more and more subtle work.

During the 1990s, I continued to practice massage therapy including CranioSacral Therapies but a series of events in my personal life were about to overshadow anything I was doing in those realms. My husband quit his job, which also provided us housing; an outside income that I had had for over ten years ended; and our son, who was age four, was diagnosed as hearing impaired. The ensuing stress of near bankruptcy and dealing with the emotional impairment of my son, that accompanied the hearing impairment, brought me to the deepest despair of my life. I was under constant emotional and mental stress that set up deep layers of tension throughout my body. Feeling restraint from all sides I went the only direction I could...within. I began to meditate daily, asking for guidance and support. Within I found the richest and most abundant spiritual energy imaginable. When life seemed to be unbearable externally, I could always count on this internal place of support, peace and solace. During one meditation, I remember surrendering my life in service, in whatever form that might be, to this sacred energy. Shortly afterward, I knew a corner had been turned and, although my life still looked difficult on the outside, it was now moving in the direction of healing and abundance.

All this occurred in Mexico where we spent our winters. My husband was born and raised in Sonora and winter was his time to be "home." Every summer we would return to Montana and I would be "home." When I returned to Montana in the spring of 1998, I discovered one of my former bodywork clients had taken some Reiki classes and was now offering energy sessions.

I knew from Reiki sessions that I had received prior to that summer that it was a great healing modality, but I had never been interested in the training for myself. After receiving Reiki from my former client, a spark of ancient recognition arose and I went in search of training. In my first level training with Reiki Master Teacher, Mary Fagan, I remember being in resistance to Reiki right up to the moment of the attunement. Then, all my deeply held memories of Reiki in past lifetimes burst open in great joy. I called my instructor after the first day of training and asked how soon could I take Reiki II! Several months after that, I completed the Reiki III training.

Fast forward to 2004. I was still using Reiki as my primary healing tool and getting ready to teach a class in Tucson. I had written this book and was about to publish it. Then during a meditation, a new healing protocol dropped into my conscious awareness. At first I thought it was a new form of Reiki, but as I worked with it I realized it was something entirely new. It worked with a new energy system that I called "Crystalline" and, as it turns out, was specifically for after the 2012 shift when the Earth moved into the New Earth energies. Its focus was on transformation versus healing (although it turned out transforming is healing as well).

And so my journey with Crystalline Consciousness Technique began. I spent years studying, experiencing and teaching it to others. In 2009, I wrote a book titled *Transformation: The Emergence of the Crystalline System*. In 2013, I wrote another book about CCT called *The Way of Transformation: Discovering the Divine Map to Unlock Your Highest Potential*. To complete the trilogy, there'll be a third book published in the near future called *Masters of Transformation*.

Unfortunately, I didn't know how Reiki fit in with CCT, the New Earth, or the Crystalline Energy System so it got parked to one side without right closure. One day, I woke with this idea that the healing system of Reiki needed to be transformed itself so that it was aligned to the New Earth. I didn't even know if my manuscript was still around but when I looked into the depths of an older computer, there it was. I'll be honest with you. I argued, and resisted and threatened to bag it all. Working with the manual as it had been was like revisiting an old time that was hard and painful. I finally threw my hands up in the air and said, "I surrender!" Meaning, I was going to scrap the whole project. The next morning, I got up and I felt I had turned some corner. Or better yet, Reiki had turned a corner. It had transformed into New Earth Reiki. Once I understood that I needed to use some of the Crystalline Consciousness Technique tools to transform Reiki, updating the book has been a delight and a surprise.

Reiki always had a special place in my heart. It led me to my purpose. With this book I want to honor it and the teachers who guided me in the Reiki system of healing. What wasn't available back in 2004 was a way to do the attunements so that they could be accessed by the reader (hard to remember those pre-technology moments in time!) This book contains links for you to listen to that will activate your own healing Reiki powers that are aligned to the New Earth.

If you are new to Reiki, this will just feel normal to you as you have nothing else to compare it to. But New Earth Reiki has a power and light to it that is way beyond normal Reiki. If you are already using Reiki, I look forward to introducing you to the Crystalline Energy System and the Crystalline Grids of the planet while giving your Reiki sessions a boost in power, joy and abundance.

We have arrived at a time in human evolution when we must understand ourselves as not just solid form in 3rd dimension, but also as energy in a multidimensional universe. Just as we need new ways of accessing energy for our homes, technology, businesses and vehicles, we need new ways, awareness and knowledge about how to maintain, protect and promote our own individual energy.

Awakening to your energetic self and innate healing powers is a joyful and fun process. It is a "remembering." In the New Earth energies, you can access your highest potential with new levels of growth. This is why we're here.

Publishing this book has been an act of time travel as I honor what brought me step by step to Crystalline Consciousness Technique. And now Crystalline Consciousness Technique brings the New Earth energies to Reiki. The spiral is complete.

Introduction

How to Use This Manual

"Our purpose in living on Earth is to bring our spiritual consciousness, which is our true nature, completely into the body." -William L. Rand

The intention of this book is to bring the wonderful realm of energy healing to anyone who is interested in becoming more active in their own healing processes and offer a potent healing tool for their own community and animal companions. It is also appropriate for people already trained in Reiki who wish to increase the power of their healing sessions. This book is not intended, however, to teach a person how to become a professional energy healer. If that is your intention, I encourage you to use this book as a great entry or doorway into this realm, but then to study with a teacher who will help you with the professional side of energy healing.

The foundation for New Earth Reiki is Usui Reiki. There are many wonderful books already in print about Usui Reiki so I just touch on its history and background briefly in the appendix.

Reiki is a form of spiritual healing also known as energy medicine or laying on of hands. Although some believe it originated with Buddhists in India as a method for achieving enlightenment, it is not a religion. Reiki is spiritual, though, and brings spiritual abundance as well as all other forms of abundance into a Reiki practitioner's life.

The Japanese word "Reiki" roughly translates to Universal Energy, which surrounds and infuses everything. A Reiki practitioner channels Universal Energy in the unique Reiki frequency through his or her body for the benefit of another person, animal or even the practitioner herself. Although we are all able to channel Universal Energy, also known as Prana, Chi, or Ki, the Reiki practitioner is able to channel this healing energy in extremely powerful ways because of the unique Reiki attunement or initiation process.

When a person is attuned to Reiki, his body's energy channels are opened and cleared of obstructions. This is healing in and of itself, as it lifts out karma or unresolved past life issues and allows for a powerful infusion of spirit, the energy of your soul. Attunements are ultimately a mystical experience that can't be fully grasped through the left brain but must be experienced to be understood. During the process the "higher" senses or psychic abilities such as clairaudience, clairvoyance and clairsentience open and become more heightened.

Besides the attunement process there are other unique features of Reiki. These include the "hot" hands of the Reiki practitioner when giving a treatment and Reiki's system of symbols that addresses healing on physical, emotional, mental, and spiritual levels. Reiki energy has consciousness and is self-directing and balancing. It is infinitely creative and combines well with other modalities and activities. Reiki flows through the body of the practitioner, bringing built-in protection for the practitioner and receiver. Other forms of energy healing don't offer such protection especially for an initiate. An old energy belief about healing is that it will drain the healer, ultimately affecting her health. Reiki enhances life, both for the healer and the receiver.

There are three levels in Reiki. Level one is for physical healing and students receive one symbol. It is appropriate for all people to use for themselves, their family, homes, and pets. Reiki II students receive two symbols, one each for emotional and mental healing. Practitioners learn distance healing with this level. Reiki III is the master level which has two more symbols, one for the spiritual body and one for the blueprint level of your Soul.

So what is New Earth Reiki? In 2012, the Earth began shifting into a new energy system. Up until then, the primary system of life was electromagnetic. After 2012, it became Crystalline. There was also a change astrologically from the Piscean age to the Aquarian. This is the shift of ages mentioned in prophecies. Our relationship to the Divine switched from being spiritual martyrs to Divine co-creators. Or to paraphrase my favorite Jimi Hendrix saying, "from the love of power to the power of love."

In energy healing, a basic tenet is the greater the power the healer holds, the greater the healing. Prior to 2012, power was defined as the amount of electromagnetic energy held in a person's energy fields that increased with spiritual expansion, growth or enlightenment.

The Crystalline Energy System holds exponentially more potential of power than the electromagnetic one. New Earth Reiki activates and works with the Crystalline Energy System increasing the power in the practitioner's energy channels and allowing for a greater flow of Reiki. Additionally, NE Reiki addresses the Crystalline Energy System as well as the electromagnetic system.

Another unique facet of New Earth Reiki is the Crystalline Energy Field in which a practitioner works. (The Crystalline Energy System is within your body, while the CE Field is all around you). This is an energy field that we strategically use to protect the aura or that space around your body that is part of your energy body. As Earth fluctuates with her magnetic shield, is bombarded by the sun, and we're affected by the distortion of electromagnetic fields created by human energy grids, our own aura needs more protection.

As Reiki moves through this crystalline energy field, the effect is significantly more powerful than in traditional forms. First level New Earth Reiki practitioners start at the power of Reiki II practitioners, while New Earth Reiki II practitioners work at the typical Reiki III level. The end results are Reiki practitioners who are more effective in their healing treatments and the ability to master the three levels of Reiki in accelerated timing.

Prior to 2012, the planet's energy was very dense. In order to connect to our souls more powerfully, we had to move up and out of our bodies. Currently the vibration of the planet with its crystalline grids is very different. In New Earth Reiki, we are more fully in our bodies than ever before, as well as conscious about our multidimensional expression. The benefits are many, including easily manifesting your soul's purpose on the planet and releasing deep levels of loneliness that came from disconnecting or forgetting your core essence. With its emphasis not only on the new Crystalline Energy System for all living beings but also the Crystalline Grids now on the planet, New Earth Reiki offers a potent tool for healing, not only ourselves, but also our planet.

How to Use This Manual

This manual is experiential as well as instructional. **When I state to stop and listen to an energy meditation, activation or attunement, please refer to your resource page.** The protocols and symbols won't work without these attunements.

If you are new to Reiki, please wait a month between Reiki Attunements I and II and II and III (essentially Chapters 5, 6, and 7). Read Chapter 5 and practice the homework given in that chapter, then a month later read Chapter 6 and practice the material in that chapter. After a month, read and practice the material in Chapter 7. If you are a Reiki Master or Level 3 Reiki practitioner, you determine your own pace and timing.

In Chapter One, you'll read more about the New Earth, the Crystalline Energy System and the Crystalline Grids. You'll be given a link to a Crystalline Energy System activation and learn why the Crystalline Energy System is so important on the planet now when it comes to healing. Be sure to listen to the activation before proceeding to the next part.

In Chapter Two, you'll learn about the Crystalline Energy Field and how to setup up or create fields to protect you energetically while also connecting you in greater harmony with others. Before the activation for the protocol for setting up fields, you'll listen to an energy meditation and receive a New Earth Reiki Symbol. This symbol will help you develop energetic integrity when you do healing as well as stay in the New Earth energies.

Chapter Three explores Energy Anatomy of the body. It is a big chapter and rather "dense." Read through it quickly then revisit it as you like. Its purpose is to prime your intuition when you are working on others.

In Chapter Four you'll learn how to heighten your intuition and connect to the Reiki Guardians. Practice muscle testing every day until it becomes second nature to you. As your intuition heightens from the Reiki attunements, you'll be able to double check your intuitive perceptions.

In Chapters Five, Six and Seven, you'll learn the three levels of New Earth Reiki with attunements, symbols and healing sessions. NE Reiki Level I in chapter 5 focuses on healing yourself, while NE Reiki Level II focuses on beginning to work with others. NE

Reiki Level III shows you how to do a distance session and work with animals. Be sure to wait at least a month between each of these chapters/levels before proceeding.

In the Appendix, you'll discover a Glossary, more resources for reading, the Usui Reiki story and how to go further with Crystalline Consciousness Technique and New Earth Reiki.

One final note: When I say "activation" you know you are learning a Crystalline Consciousness Technique tool while "attunement" is a Reiki tool.

Are you ready to start your journey into becoming a healer in the New Earth energies? Let's get started!

Chapter One

The New Earth

"You know the world is a magical place when Mother Earth grows her own jewelry." -Dr. Athena Perrakis

This is an exciting time on the planet. After the shift of 2012, the planet began to develop crystalline grids which became complete in 2017. Prior to 2012, Gaia or Mother Earth began preparing for this leap in transformation or evolution by calling in the Indigos, Starseed, Rainbow and Crystalline souls. These souls have one thing in common—a fully activated Crystalline Energy System. At the time they began arriving in the 1980s, most humans and other life operated from their electromagnetic energy system. That gradually changed then accelerated after 2012 when Earth also transformed. More and more people developed a Crystalline Energy System, either spontaneously or through some other form of transformation.

Besides the new Crystalline Energy System, New Earth energies arise from a combination of the Aquarian Age, the Crystalline Grids and Crystalline Field. All together they create amazing new potentials on the planet such as rapid healing, releasing distortions in the biofield (such as cancer cells), using fewer resources, and finding solutions for problems like radiation, global warming, pollution, etc. To fully understand the New Earth and how to operate within its highest potential is still an unfolding story, but the most important aspect is to be in the New Earth energies.

Stepping into the New Earth energies is easy. Stand up, take one step to the right, and state your intention to be in the New Earth energies. It's a subtle shift but you may immediately feel lighter and more joyful. When you imagine you're looking toward the future it will seem brighter and you'll feel more hopeful. The Crystalline Energy System is ideal for operating in the New Earth so let's stop and jump right in with your first activation. **Stop and Listen to Your First Activation on the Resource Page.**

Energy Concepts

Before explaining the advantages of the Crystalline Energy System over the electromagnetic energy system when it comes to healing, let's first cover some basic energy concepts:

Everything is energy

First energy, then form

Shift the energy and the form will follow

Energy responds to your intent

We notice energy through our emotions, mental moods and senses

Observing energy lets you work directly with energy

Everyone observes energy through a unique signature perception

The Advantages of the Crystalline Energy System

You may be wondering how the body created a crystalline energy system. The body (and Earth) has been evolving forever. Our brain started with a reptilian brain, then developed a limbic brain, then a frontal brain. Often this occurs during the moment of conception. It's as though Earth speaks to the heavens and says, "I need life to be ready for this next stage." Then the souls ready for that new level of expression appear ready for incarnation. For people (and animals) already alive, the transformative process can be more painful as well as disorienting.

To help with this, activations or attunements have been created. The activation creates an alchemical tipping point with your connective tissue, water element and the mineral salts in your body. A new system, greater than its parts seems to magically appear. You become a walking crystalline matrix with all kinds of cool upgrades. Before we explore the reasons why you want a Crystalline Energy System, let's take a moment and explain what an energy system does.

The body has many kinds of organ systems, each one with its own job description. Through, around, and within each of these different organ systems is your energy body whose job is to create unity between all the different organ systems, transfer information and determine how outside energy is going to affect inside organs. It also orders and organizes external energy for the body to use (like a tree bringing in sunshine through its leaves and nutrients up through its roots). An energy information system interprets, orders and organizes energy and feeds that information/energy to the organs. The higher vibrational and more coherent the energy information system is, the more it can create health and growth at a rapid pace (think old dial up internet versus high speed wi fi).

Generally, when Earth evolves it builds on prior systems but the transformation that happened in 2012 was different. In the spiritual community, the predictions were all about ascending from 3rd dimensional awareness to 5th dimensional awareness...or enlightened consciousness. Earth chose to evolve a new energy system first. Her strategy is brilliant because the new energy system addresses problems that existed in the electromagnetic energy system. We couldn't get where we need to be from where we were for a vital, sustainable, healthy planet. Here are 9 reasons why we need a Crystalline Energy System:

1. **Instant Enlightenment**: The electromagnetic energy system is too slow for the current rate of transformation. If too much energy enters to quickly through the EM system, it will blow circuits. The CE system can deal with tremendous amounts of energy very quickly. Translated into spiritual terms, you can become enlightened immediately instead of spending decades or lifetimes preparing yourself for this level of soul development.
2. **Release Karmic Entanglement:** Have you ever struggled to release an old pattern or connections to certain toxic people, but they just seem to come back again and again? Or have you ever noticed how certain group patterns take so long to transform (issues such as racism, dishonesty in politics, greed in businesses or disempowerment of women)? These issues have become entangled energetically in the electromagnetic energy systems. It's like a big knot that gets more tangled the more you try to detangle it. The complexity of this "knotted" energy reached such a critical mass that the planet couldn't transform, so it dumped the whole mess and

started over again.

3. **Works with Sacred Geometry to Order and Organize:** The CE System is a crystalline matrix which has the ability to organize tremendous amounts of energy into very ordered shapes through sacred geometry, the building blocks of life. Our CE system isn't solid but is liquid crystalline (the 4th state of water) The more ordered and organized energy is in harmonic ratios, the more vital our health.
4. **Ability to Release Distortion**: Our current health problems and challenges are distortions from the original human blueprints. A cancer cell is a healthy cell that has become distorted. Organs malfunctioning (such as heart disease or diabetes) are distortions in the blueprints. The CE System rapidly releases distortions.
5. **New Levels of Telepathy:** The CE system is able to connect to the Crystalline Energy Field all around us and heighten all forms of mental telepathy, including animal communication. It's amazingly easy and so fun.
6. **New Levels of Joy:** Joy becomes a natural state of expression as the golden ratio is built into the CE system. Love, when converted to a ratio, is the golden ratio and joy is an indicator that one is in highest level of unconditional love or agape.
7. **Out Beyond Good or Evil:** The polarity of good versus evil arose during the Piscean age and the electromagnetic system (electro is light and magnetic is dark). In the CE System and New Earth, both light and dark are neutral energies working together in co-creation.
8. **New Levels of Human Potential:** The CE System allows for accelerated learning and growing, greatly needed in a world that is shifting so rapidly.
9. **Energetic Integrity:** When out-of-integrity humans manipulate, psychically attack, or cord into each other to take energy, it creates lasting damage on many levels. The CE System avoids these energetic traps.

In the next chapter, you'll learn how to work with the Crystalline Energy Field that lies all around us to protect your energy and set the stage for New Earth Reiki.

Chapter Two

Setting Up Fields

"The key to freedom is to be fully in your body."

-Peggy Phoenix Dubro

We've talked about the emerging Crystalline Energy System within you, but now we're going to talk about the energy around you. Every single organism has an energy field that extends into the space around it, from the simplest single-celled algae to the complex human body. This energy field protects the organism like a skin.

This field or aura is dynamic and responds to both internal as well as external stimuli. It can collapse in around you when you are lacking vital life force because of an illness. It can expand out for miles when you are in nature and feeling exuberant and joyful. Culturally, Japanese and other densely populated countries keep a very quiet and small energy field. Leaders who hold a great deal of authority will often have a "larger than life" energy field as they hold a tremendous amount of space around them.

Your energy field can be damaged or become less effective for you for many reasons, including environmental, psychological, emotional, and physical ones. The energy field can be torn, ripped, too porous, or distorted. It can become stagnant, if it fails to fully assimilate or transmute toxic energies.

Once your energy field becomes compromised, your other body systems must pick up the slack, leaving them less energy to do what they are meant to be doing. The integrity of your body organs and systems can begin to breakdown.

In James L. Oshman's book, *Energy Medicine*, he refers to conditions that can happen with an impaired or damaged energy field. Depending on the degree of damage in the aura, a person can develop other physical and behavioral problems including:

- Allergies
- Chronic Fatigue Syndrome
- Sleep apnea
- Migraines
- Balance issues
- Bacterial growth
- Seizures, convulsions and epilepsy
- Adrenal failure
- Cardiovascular problems
- Weight gain
- Respiratory problems including asthma
- Anxiety
- Depression
- Loss of attention and memory
- Accidents

The solution to protect your aura involves a grid of energy called the Crystalline Energy Field. Before you learn the solution, let's talk about this field.

The Crystalline Energy Field

Extending around us is a grid of energy called the Crystalline Energy Field. It's been called other things, notably Indra's Net. If you were born with a Crystalline Energy System already activated, you are well aware of this grid of energy on an energetic level and might have used it for telepathic communication.

To bring this energetic connection to your conscious awareness (or to create an energetic connection to this field), just do the following exercise: Read the ancient description of Indra's Net, below (preferably out loud). Before starting, however, try a simple experiment to palpate the Crystalline Field.

Place your hands in the air in front of you with your awareness in your fingertips. Move your hands back and forth. If you feel a slight pulling or pushing, this is the field. Now read the description of Indra's Net and then repeat the exercise to see if it's more noticeable to you. (Don't worry...if you don't "feel" anything. That may not be your primary mode of perception. Periodically check back throughout this course and you'll find you've naturally improved.)

> **Indra's Net**
>
> Far away in the heavenly abode of the great god Indra, there is a wonderful net which has been hung by some cunning creator in such a manner that it stretches out infinitely in all directions. In accordance with the extravagant tastes of deities, the creator has hung a single glittering jewel in each "eye" of the net, and since the net itself is infinite in dimension, the jewels are infinite in number. There hang the jewels, glittering like stars in the first magnitude, a wonderful site to behold. If we now arbitrarily select one of these jewels for inspection and look closely at it, you will discover that in its polished surface there are reflected all the other jewels in the net, infinite in number. Not only that, but each of the jewels reflected in this one jewel is also reflecting all the other jewels so that there is an infinite reflecting process occurring.
>
> ~Avatamsaka Sutra

Welcome to the Crystalline Energy Field! The reason it's also called a grid of energy is that there are energy lines that run vertically and horizontally through it just like a net. They respond to vibration, like guitar strings being strummed. In New Earth Reiki, you'll use a protocol to "set up your CE field." This field of vibrating energy acts as a mirror to your own aura. Because of the laws of vibration your aura will vibrate to that high vibration. Essentially you create an energy field of higher vibration to protect your energy field.

How Vibration Helps an EM Field

Everything vibrates. Both Eastern and Western religious traditions state that sound, i.e. vibration, was present at the beginning of Creation. When vibrations are at one frequency we hear sound, when they are at higher frequencies we see light. Our normal electromagnetic energies (which we still have and work with even with a Crystalline Energy

System) have different vibrational frequencies that create a spectrum. The higher the spectrum of our energy field the higher the "light" we emanate.

Using high vibrational frequencies has another positive side effect. According to Freddy Silva in *Secrets in the Field*, "Since the human body itself is a set of atoms vibrating at a certain frequency, our ability to consciously distinguish other dimensions is limited, and like a radio station it only detects those vibrations which fall along its narrow band-width." Silva is saying that when you are attuned to high vibrations you automatically tune out lower frequencies. In the case of health, selective hearing can be a good thing.

When you set up a crystalline energy field of vibration, it acts as a mirror radiating that vibration to your aura creating a resonation effect. To get a better idea of this, imagine that there is a guitar lying in front of you. It's quiet and silent until you pick it up and strum a chord on it. The strings then vibrate according to the chord that you played. Eventually, the strings will return to their resting state if no other chords are played. This is exactly how the crystalline energy field works. Our version of strumming a guitar is to place a vibrational element (strumming the guitar) in the crystalline field and it will vibrate to that "chord" for a certain amount of time. The time is variable for different people. If you have weak or damaged energy fields, you'll have to set up your crystalline field more frequently. Doing so allows your aura to heal and repair. Eventually once or twice a day will be enough.

There are a couple of important points to understand about the Crystalline Energy Field. First, as stated in the parable of Indra's net, it is a high vibrational grid of energy lines and it is infinite with no discernible beginning or ending. You need to use very high vibrational elements to work with it. We use vibrational components from Crystalline Consciousness Technique that are extremely high in vibration and perfectly match the New Earth energies.

The second point about the CE field being infinite means that it is neutral to all form. We need to make it specific to us for it to protect our EM field. The CE field protocol addresses this and creates entrainment or resonation in the aura, a naturally occurring phenomena in the universe.

To understand entrainment, let's return to the guitar example. If there are various guitars or stringed instruments in a room and you strum a chord on one of them, the others will begin to vibrate to that chord...all by themselves! That's resonation or entrainment. In the book, *Sync: How Order Emerges from Chaos in the Universe, Nature and Daily Life*, author Steven Strogatz takes the reader through the emerging science of synchrony. He explains how we all synchronize from heart beats to brain waves to galaxies and beyond. When setting up a CE field, you will make good use of this universal dynamic.

Setting up a crystalline energy field to protect your aura is easy. You will use a protocol of statements that place vibrational elements from Crystalline Consciousness Technique in the field. Energy responds to a statement of intent. For example, if you have too much energy in your head and tell it to move to your feet, it will respond. If you tell your energy field to expand, it will (unless there is not enough vital life energy in the body system to respond). You can find an explanation of the vibrational components from CCT that we use to set up the Crystalline Energy Field in the Appendix, but first let's review the Laws of Vibration:

Laws of Vibration

All energy vibrates
Vibration resonates and synchronizes with other vibrations
High vibration creates health
Low vibration creates illness
Thoughts and words are vibrational

There's one more piece to bring to all of this before you learn the protocol for setting up your Crystalline Energy Fields and that's how to create energetic integrity.

Energetic Integrity and the New Earth Reiki Symbol

One of my favorite things I learned in massage school was how to align to gravity. To be truthful, I wasn't quite sure what we were doing back then but it felt great. With a simple inhale we imagined energy coming up from the Earth and flowing up our front to above our heads, then circling down our backs while we exhaled. It felt like being pressed between two panes of glass. What it was doing was creating energetic integrity so that we didn't project our traumas, wounds or judgements on to someone else. In New Earth Reiki, you will do something similar but in a different way. During an energy meditation, you'll receive a New Earth Reiki Symbol that is placed above and slightly in front of you. Then each of your primary energies is connected to that symbol. Besides creating energetic integrity with the psychic, heart and creative energies, the symbol reminds your Energy Body to work with the New Earth energies.

Before going further, take a moment now and listen to the energy meditation to receive your New Earth Reiki Symbol which includes instructions for connecting your 3 primary energies to the symbol.

Individual and Group Fields

The protocol that you are about to learn is for both your individual and group energies. This is one of the ways humans operated differently from other animals. Cats are predominantly individual while dogs or horse are primarily group energies. Humans are both but often we are really good with one while not so good with the other. This protocol helps you find that balance. The individual field protects you while the group field connects you in greater harmony to those you are working or living with. This protects your senses from overwhelm (think crowded, noisy restaurant or mall) and you can begin to access the wisdom of a group and its higher potential of functioning.

In this manual, you'll learn the basic protocol. In the Advanced Reiki Training there is an advanced form of this protocol that works with the Crystalline Energy System Chakras.

Tips for Setting Up Your CE Field

- Make sure you listen to the activation first (see below for the link) or the protocol won't work.
- Read the protocol as quickly as you would like, all the way through, exactly as it is written. Once the protocol is memorized it only takes seconds each day to set up your crystalline energy field.

- Set up your CE field daily, in the morning. If you have trouble sleeping, set it up at night with the specific intention of deep, restorative sleep.
- If you have a chronic illness, you will want to set up your CE field 4-6 times a day, the first three weeks. This is because your energy field is not very strong.
- If you experience strong emotional outbursts or frights during the day, set up your CE field again.
- Place the written protocol in locations where you know you'll spend some time (the bathroom, your car, beside your bed) to remind you to do it.
- This technique can be subtle! You may not notice any change until the day you forget to set up your CE field.

Before continuing, please listen to the activation for this protocol. Once finished go ahead and read the protocol. Then repeat every day.

> Get more techniques for Setting Up Your Fields such as clearing food, furniture such as mattresses or rooms from stagnant or toxic energies (such as in hotels); and protection for your car in traffic in the Advanced New Earth Reiki Training.

Protocol for Setting Up Crystalline Energy Fields

Step 1: Connect to your New Earth Reiki Symbol with your 3 primary energies. You can visualize this or state it.

Step 2: State your intention to stay protected and connected in harmony in the New Earth Energies.

Step 3: Define who's in your group (family, business, receiver of healing sessions, etc). Then state silently or out loud:

- "I ask to place the vibration of Opening in my individual crystalline energy field and my crystalline group field.
- I ask to place the Healing Chambers in my individual crystalline energy field and my crystalline group field in the appropriate order for my day (or this healing session).
- I ask to place the vibration of my Intention in my individual crystalline energy field and my crystalline group field.
- I ask to place the vibration of the 23 crystal vibrations in my individual crystalline energy field and my crystalline group field.
- I ask to place the vibration of Mastery in my individual crystalline energy field and my crystalline group field.
- I ask to connect to the Crystalline Grids of the Planet.
- I ask to connect to the Crystalline Energy Field."

Chapter Three

Energy Anatomy

"The day science begins to study non-physical phenomena, it will make more progress in one decade than in all the previous centuries of its existence." –Nikola Tesla

We've already talked about some of our energy anatomy including the aura, the Crystalline Energy System (within you) and the Crystalline Energy field (around you). In this chapter we'll cover other types of energy anatomy, which is vast and complex, full of currents and vortexes, layers and levels, frequencies and vibrations, rhythms and pulsations. All of these must integrate and stay in synchronization with impulses of energy from your soul as well as impulses from the planet. Since the rise of technology in the past century and a half, we are also being inundated with man-made impulses that are out of sync with natural rhythms. If Reiki did nothing but help synchronize all the rhythms in the body, it would be a great service, but of course Reiki does much more as well.

In this chapter, I provide some basic concepts for the novice as well as certain information that is unique to New Earth Reiki. Reading this chapter begins to entrain your higher sense perceptions to consciously read energy and provides context for some of the healing techniques found in this book. Techniques to address energy anatomy issues are explained in later chapters.

When reading different books about energy anatomy, there seems to be conflicting descriptions. There are different energy systems that overlap each other and some that don't seem to overlap at all. Most of what is recorded comes from higher sense perceptions. Intuitive energy reading can change depending from the level from which it is perceived. The recent vibrational change in the planet has not only brought changes to the energy fields, but also our ability to perceive more than in the past. When you begin your own journey of reading energy anatomy, you'll want to factor that in. Use the information in this and other books as a general road map, validating your own observations, but not limiting them.

Energy Body

The Energy Body is a term used in New Earth Reiki that refers to a field of energy through and around the body that contains the innate wisdom of the body. It responds to intentions and thoughts and is actively dynamic with the healing mechanisms in the body. The Energy Body has its own consciousness, aware of what needs to heal and what order the healing should occur in. After a Reiki receiver has discussed his focus, I silently ask his Energy Body what it wants to work on, what type of work it wants, as well as the order in which the work is presented. The Energy Body can also communicate when to allow time for assimilating or completing an energy process and when to stop.

Sometimes all the Energy Body is missing is information. As facilitators of energy healing, we can provide a lens or mirror in which to reflect that information to the Energy Body. As soon as the Energy Body receives the information, it will begin to work on and through the body. To the practitioner this can be felt as an unwinding through the whole body system and needs only be supported and observed while it is occurring.

There are times when the Energy Body isn't seated correctly in the body. I perceive it as if it was turned backward. This causes reverse magnetic polarity in the body. In this state, what normally strengthens the body now weakens it. In a child, this condition shows up in a type of mood traditionally called "getting up on the wrong side of the bed." When the Energy Body is seated backward it causes everything to flow backward, including meridians, and causes us to push away that which we are intending to draw in. Usually the Energy Body will seat itself in correct polarity by just asking it to do so.

If a simple "request" doesn't get the Energy Body to turn around, the cause can be an emotional attachment to something or someone in the past. Unfinished emotional work around that person or event in the past, or not letting go of someone who has died, are two main causes of untimely attachments. If our reference point for the person who has died stays attached to the form (which now only exists in the past), instead of the spirit, then the Energy Body will orient itself backward. What's needed is to relocate the reference point from the past to the present by connecting to that person's spirit in whatever dimension he or she is in now. This rarely works, however, if a person is still in an active grieving process. Then all that is called for is emotional support and witnessing of the grief.

Other causes for the Energy Body to flip backward can be environmental stressors, including fluorescent lights, or exposure to electromagnetic fields such as computers, cars, airplanes and other machines.

Communicating with the Energy Body is easy. Using intention to link with the Energy Body, I ask it yes/no questions. For answers, I use muscle testing, which is covered in Chapter Four. Often after I ask a question, I'll be shown visually where to start or where to go next.

Subtle Bodies

As energy steps down from the highest vibrational level of your soul into your 3rd dimensional body, it can be categorized into the subtle bodies of spiritual, mental, emotional and physical. Reiki symbols are often associated with one of these four levels, but this is a very one-dimensional way of seeing energy anatomy. Within each level exists components of all other levels. For example, in the physical body lies the central nervous system which connects with the mental body; the organs and the limbic center in the brain which are often centers of emotions; and the spiritual body which creates a unified energy field of purpose or forward direction among all the components and systems of the physical body. It is limiting to Reiki symbols to think that Sei He Ki is only an emotional body symbol or that Cho Ku Rei is for physical body only.

To make it all a bit more complex each energy body has another energy body that is vibrationally an octave higher. The physical body has the etheric body, the emotional body has the astral body, the mental body has the mental grid, and the spiritual body has the causal body. Blueprints or templates for the physical, emotional, mental and spiritual bodies are found in the throat energy center.

In addition to the subtle bodies, there are transformers that help step down the energy and connect one body with the next. These channels can get blocked causing disconnection within the energetic bodies. This can lead to the physical body having a separate intention from the emotional or mental body and all three of these can be at odds with the spiritual body. Any place where there is conflict within the body creates an underlying tension which can lead to dis-ease if the conflict isn't resolved. Mental body conflicts can show up in psychological discord but so can spiritual and physical disharmonies. Mental and emotional conflicts can manifest physically. A deep spiritual conflict can show up in a chronic illness. Conflict can also show up externally in a person's life as well, such as in the areas of relationships, money, and career.

Disconnected energy bodies lead to a lack of integrity. Integration or wholeness is the foundation for integrity. One of the most confusing types of people are the ones who mentally communicate one thing, emotionally another and physically another. Our own energy fields can end up being muddled and more confused when we are around this type of person. Before I understood these energetics, my body would let me know immediately if a person was being aggressive on an energetic level and not owning it consciously. I would experience a very powerful, fast and reactive type of anger. Initially this confused me as it never seemed related to what the person was saying. As I began to understand energy better, I realized anger clears the energy field of manipulative or hooking energy and sets boundaries. Anger became my indicator signal when there were boundary issues.

When we have energy bodies that aren't aligned in purpose, we become deeply ineffectual in our lives. We don't achieve our potential and frustration builds up within us. By anchoring our soul's highest purpose as the primary organizing dynamic, through all of our energy bodies, then all levels can work toward the same intention.

The energy of trauma has an interesting effect on our subtle bodies. If trauma overwhelms us on one level, then it will move into another level. This is one of the ways karma is created. Trauma that reaches the spiritual body and is not resolved is carried into the next lifetime. Each time trauma moves into another subtle body, it causes secondary effects through all the bodies. When working with a person it may take several sessions to work through all the effects of trauma before getting to the actual primary lesion or energy cyst. The benefit of healing in this manner, though, is that once all of these layers are released they are gone for good.

° **Physical Body:** The physical body is the densest of the four subtle bodies. It contains the Kundalini chakras, grounding cord, and meridians. Chakras are covered more in depth later in the chapter and the Grounding Cord is discussed under Vertical Energies.

The physical and spiritual bodies have a close relationship with each other as do the mental and emotional bodies. Rarely are they out of harmony. Thus the soul often speaks through physical symptoms. If we can honor body symptoms as a soul message instead of resisting them, or condemning them, we can begin to shape shift the symptoms into more "comfortable" ways.

During times of extreme trauma or adversity, anger or fear, our physical body constricts. This causes muscles to contract cutting off oxygen from the muscle tissue. Without oxygen a muscle cannot relax and it squeezes the nerves. The nerves transfer their distress to the mind, which then becomes the stressed mind. Our ability to respond and to make conscious choices becomes limited and restricted as our musculoskeletal system feels pain and tension and our mind feels stress and distress. Ultimately the well-being of the entire organism is threatened.

One sign of the muscles relaxing after an energy healing treatment is extreme tiredness. Encourage your receiver to rest for a while after a session.

° **Emotional Body**: A very fluid body, the emotional body includes the emotions, which simply are energy in motion; the Hara Line; and part of the Silver Cord (which allows us to astral travel and receive higher soul levels into the body). Both the Hara Line and the Silver Cord are discussed under Vertical Energies.

When the emotional body is like a clear stream that flows deeply and smoothly, it becomes a powerful part of our informational system as well as providing us the means to manifest our soul's purpose. When emotions aren't expressed or processed completely, they are stored in our physical, mental, or spiritual bodies. During healing, these emotions are freed and begin to move through us. Suddenly we can be assaulted by overwhelming grief, anger, resistance or fear. By placing awareness upon the breath and the movement within the body as one inhales and exhales, the emotions are encouraged to move all the way through the energetic bodies. The mind becomes clear and the body feels emptied out, allowing for greater synthesis throughout the organism.

Those who have emotional intelligence are often empathic. They feel what others are feeling. This can be overwhelming, if the pain of others' emotions is taken into their bodies. Reiki, with its vertical flow of energy moving into the practitioner's body then horizontally to the receiver, helps correct and balance empaths from being overwhelmed and to release emotions that aren't their own.

- **Anger**: The potent emotions of anger and fear are part of our protective mechanisms. Anger, as already mentioned, fills our field with fiery energy burning through restrictions and inappropriate energy from others. We do not need to do anything with anger, neither directing it toward others, nor ourselves. Instead all that is required is to let it fill our field, creating healthy boundaries and notifying our conscious minds of boundary or integrity issues. When anger moves into the mental body, it becomes resentment. Anger that moves into the spiritual level turns to rage.
- **Fear**: Fear heightens our intuition and asks us to take some form of action (fight, flight or freeze to avoid confrontation). It can be a powerful ally when we are in right relationship to fear. Worry is a form of fear that is projected into the future. It constricts energy channels and doesn't allow our best possible outcomes to manifest. Those who tend to worry need to practice staying fully in the present, grounding to a greater degree and increasing trust. Fear moving into the mental body becomes anxiety. Nonspecific anxiety can often be created when our energy fields are not clear and our Energy Body picks up information on some level that it is not able to interpret or understand. Anxiety asks us to become clearer vessels so that discernment may be used for appropriate action for what is requiring attention. When fear moves into the spiritual level it becomes terror and we are frozen in immobility. It is easy in this state to have a piece of the soul fracture off and stay immobilized, stuck out of time and space. Locating these pieces and integrating them is known as soul retrieval. The Reiki symbol called Dai Ko Myo can help integrate soul fragments.

- **Depression**: Depression is another emotion that is a powerful messenger. It asks that we withdraw our energy from the external world and go deeply within to retrieve some part of ourselves or reorganize on all levels. The fear around depression is that if we let ourselves sink within we'll never come out of that hole. In actuality, the less we resist depression and trust its message, the sooner it will reverse its flow. Depression in the mental body becomes apathy and affects the will to live. This in turn causes chemical imbalances and impairs the immune system. Depression that moves into the spiritual level becomes despair.
- **Grief**: Grief is a complicated emotion that can include anger, depression, joy and sadness. It has its own sense of timing. When it's over, it's over and not before then. Grief can get stuck from completion when we try to stay linked to the past to whomever or whatever we are grieving and not let go of the old form when it is time.

A client, Sara, came to me about her chronic bronchitis. Sara's unresolved grief and conflicting emotions about the passing of her grandfather manifested in an interesting way. Sara had loved her grandfather dearly when she was young but then as a young adult watched him deteriorate into alcoholism. She became angry and disdainful about her grandfather and wouldn't let herself grieve both losses that she sustained with her grandfather. The energy of unacknowledged grief went deep into the energy field of the microbes in her body. The microbes took on the "role" of expressing the unowned grief by creating constant lung ailments. By addressing the grief consciously and then clearing the microbe's energy field, Sara was able to improve her health and acknowledge the positive parts of her relationship with her grandfather.

Unresolved grief in the mental body can show up as disappointment and unhappiness with life. If unresolved grief moves into the spiritual body, it can manifest in the next lifetime through an aura of sadness, as though the person carries around his own rain cloud of gloom.

- **Joy**: Joy is the natural state of being when a high level of harmony exists on all levels. Joy in the mental body is happiness. On the spiritual level, joy is felt as ecstasy or bliss. This state is achieved when the pineal gland is infused with spiritual energy, a natural occurrence of enlightenment and other types of awakenings. Bliss is extremely healing if anchored through all the other subtle bodies. Joy is a natural consequence or indicator of the spiritual state of unconditional love.

- **Love**: Although love is generally described as an emotion, it is in a class all its own. It is one of the qualities of Divine Order that is woven through the deepest fibers of our entire being. Tom Kenyon, an extraordinary sound healer, on his CD titled *The Ghandarva Ceremony*, talks about an Australian pianist/scientist who noted that when he touched the piano keys with a certain amount of pressure it invoked the same feelings throughout his audience no matter what type of music he was playing. He developed a machine to measure the different emotions through pressure. Translating the data into ratios, love was discovered to be the same ratio as the golden means. Part of sacred geometry, the golden means ratio is a building block in Nature, including in the spiral of DNA. When we feel or express love we actually strengthen and repair our DNA. The statement that love heals is not a fuzzy, warm platitude but a powerful truth for all of us to know.

° **Mental Body**: The mental body is extremely powerful containing the individual mind, brain and central nervous system, thoughts, and belief systems. The mental body takes the pure essence of being and through the focus and direction of thoughts manifests what we call reality. Thoughts are energy grids for form. We manifest very powerfully when these energy grids are magnetized with emotions. Some energy grids that the mind creates can be destructive, not life enhancing. Psychic attacks are negative thoughts either in the conscious or the subconscious mind that energetically targets the person we are focused on. They can cause energetic damage to that person and karma for the one psychically attacking. Although we like to think we have only been the receivers of psychic attack, the odds are that we have also been the senders. A person with a controlling mind literally throws an energy field around the person he or she is trying to force to a certain outcome.

The psychological term "projection," meaning to project an unaccepted quality of oneself onto another person, is an energetic phenomenon as well. Many couples act out each other's unaccepted psychological parts never realizing they are not their own!

Conversely, thoughts of prayer, gratitude and affirmation create expansive positive energy that create healing for ourselves and others.

Belief systems are thoughts that have become part hidden to our conscious awareness, similar to the operating system in a computer. Formed during certain developmental stages, belief systems should be examined periodically to see if they still serve us. Oftentimes we can only know our belief systems by what we create in our lives. Mass consciousness is a collective form of cultural, social and family belief systems affecting us on all levels. As we spiritually evolve we can vibrate at a higher rate than mass consciousness and no longer be affected by it.

If the emotional body has emotions, the mental body has moods. These can be created from emotions such as depression or joy and from physical body chemistry. As mentioned earlier, if the Energy Body is seated backward in the body it can create a very dark mood. Moods can also be created when we are unconscious about our mind and the way it works. The mind constantly creates thoughts that can be critical, defeating or negative. Monkey mind, as it is referred to in Eastern religions, never stops. Meditation is a powerful tool for becoming the master of our minds instead of being enslaved by them. *Breathwalk*, by Gurucharan Sing Khalsa and Yogi Bhajan gives an excellent technique for working with the mind through breath rhythms and walking. Becoming mindfully aware is also a powerful technique presented in *The Power of Now* by Eckart Tolle.

The powerful energy stream of the mental body, also known as psychic energy, needs to be harnessed and directed in a positive way or it will create problems within the body. It works best when tempered by inspiration from the spiritual body, positive emotions from the emotional body, and focus and concentration in partnership with the physical body. The ultimate quality for health is a quiet mind that is positive, clear, detached, focused, directed, and always curious.

° **Spiritual Body**: Surrounding and infusing our denser bodies as well as extending out through many levels of the soul, our spiritual body is about empowered and higher levels of wisdom that span both past and future. Harder to discern within ourselves, the spiritual body is like a beautiful tone that after a while we no longer hear. Just as when the tone suddenly stops and we notice it by its absence, if the connection to our spiritual body stops we can become overwhelmed by despair. If this shows up physically, we can experience a host of symptoms that doctors can't identify, regardless of how many tests they administer. All symptoms of disease begin at the spiritual body. If this level is addressed first, then the other levels will respond to more traditional approaches or will clear by themselves.

To grow spiritually is to receive an energy infusion from our soul through the body. As energy also carries information, then we are able to suddenly understand the way the universe works from higher levels of consciousness. This is the realm of the mystic. Ultimately, if we hold the triune of spiritual expansion equally through mental, emotional and spiritual bodies, it will lead us to the illumined soul, enlightened mind and the beloved heart or agape.

Chakras

Chakras are energy vortexes or centers. There are 7 main ones in traditional energy anatomy and 5 associated with the Crystalline Energy System. Chakras hold information from the soul, help organize energy as it enters the body and provide a road map for personality and soul development. Our personality is part of the housing and protection mechanism for our soul. As it develops it is capable of holding more spiritual power. Usually the completion of a personality developmental stage is accompanied by an increase in spiritual energy or an infusion of soul. If the personality gets stopped developmentally at any one stage, it becomes out of sync with the natural stages of soul infusion. Too much spiritual energy into the body when we're not ready blows circuits, while not enough spiritual energy into our system creates stagnation.

The seven developmental stages or themes relating to the chakras are: Survival, Belonging, Power, Love, Expression, Wisdom, and Unity. Each chakra's theme has both personal and transpersonal qualities for the personality and the soul. For example, the

Solar Plexus chakra relates to power. This implies both self-esteem and Soul's worth. Although we can be working on any of the chakra themes at any time, they correspond with our biological growth as well. Because there are seven main chakras it has been thought that each stage lasts seven years. Interestingly the stage of Power, which traditionally lasted from 14-21 years of age, is almost twice as long in the American culture. Whether this is because our school systems are disempowering, or if we as a society are frightened of the level of power that teenagers have and try to disempower them, or if this period is extending longer because we are living longer, the answer is not fully known at this time.

Chakras have physical, emotional, mental and spiritual components. On the physical level certain organs, glands, nerve plexus, muscles, tendons and ligaments all correspond to the chakra, generally the one they are closest to. Each chakra also has a primary emotion that is associated with it. The mental components with each chakra are about sensory perception and knowledge. The spiritual components are about informing from spiritual levels.

Developmental Tasks in Chakras

Personal Tasks		Transpersonal Tasks
1st	Sense of belonging tribally/culturally	DNA memories of all cultures
2nd	Sense of belonging through family	Creating community
3rd	Value self/self-worth	Know and value soul's worth
4th	Love self	Love others unconditionally
5th	Balance giving and receiving	Master duality
6th	Develop discernment	Master free will/choice at soul level
7th	Own individual spirituality	Unity Consciousness

Traditionally each chakra has a certain color associated with it. These colors don't reflect the actual colors of the chakras, which are multi-colored, or that the chakra requires that color for healing. Instead the vibrational meaning of each color represents a certain quality or feel of that chakra.

The areas where chakras overlap can get extremely congested. Physically these areas are the diaphragms and nerve plexus of the body. Four physical diaphragms are between the Root and Sexual/Creative chakras, Solar Plexus and Heart, Heart and Throat, Throat and Third Eye. A fifth diaphragm is located in the Throat at the hyoid bone. The sixth diaphragm is an energetic one between Sexual/Creative and Solar Plexus chakras. In Oriental Medicine it is referred to as the belt channel. These crossover areas are also portals into other dimensions.

In healing, Reiki addresses the seven main chakras, also known as the Kundalini or Physical Body Chakras. In the Advanced New Earth Reiki Training we address seven levels within each of these chakras as well. Each level represents or echoes the corresponding chakra. These are called chakra complexes. As with all of our energetic anatomy the chakras work best when linked with each other through all levels.

° **Base Chakra** (*First; Survival*): Located at the tip of the coccyx on men and the tip of the cervix for women, this energy center is associated with red, the color of physical strength and life vitality. The large intestines as well as the reptilian brain are closely linked with this chakra. When experiences in life seem to strip us down to the pure essence of life, we experience the basic, pure drive of the base chakra.

The emotional component of the base chakra is fear. The mental component is the sense of awe of life, such as we feel in the presence of a birth. The spiritual component is attainment—that moment when what we have intended to manifest comes into form.

Energetically the base chakra is part of our grounding mechanism. When we are in fear we disconnect our energy from the ground. This chakra also deals with tribal energies and memories, including our cultural roots, and with a survival level of living. Male sexual energy is seated in this chakra unless a man has chosen a spiritual path and reseated this energy in the second chakra. Both the base chakra and the sexual/creative chakra love drumming.

° **Sexual/Creative Chakra** (*Second; Creation*): Located in the pelvic bowl, this chakra is the seat of our creative energies. For women it is the seat of sexual energy as well. Its color association is the emotionally uplifting color of orange. It is linked to the reproductive organs and glands and the sacrum—the seat of the Kundalini energy. Its primary emotion is passion. The spiritual component is desire, as to create anything it first must be desired. When we existed in the void, the great womb of creative empowerment, some spark that came from the Divine Creator itself suddenly moved through us and we expanded into form.

There is no mental component with this chakra. The sexual/creative chakra relates to family, community and money. In its purest form money is just energy. Because of its neutrality we can project all sorts of issues that we might have on money.

People who have potent sexual/creative chakras are highly charismatic or magnetic. Shamans heal with this energy. If a person was a healer in past lives, that energy links very strongly with the creative energy. Like mental body energy, the healing/creative energy needs external focus and direction or it can create unwanted conditions in our life as it works subconsciously.

We have a unique connection to the moon through our second chakra. In *The Woman's Book of Dreams* by Connie Kaplan, she talks about energy fibers that connect women's wombs to the moon. As the moon moves every month through the different signs in astrology, it invokes a certain vibration that influences what type of dreams we have. Men who identify with their receptivity or feminine energies can activate these fibers, which connect into their second chakras.

° **Solar Plexus Chakra** (*Third; Power*): Located above the navel and below the sternum notch, the solar plexus chakra is associated with the color of yellow, a color known for creating self-confidence. It's connected to all of the digestive organs, liver, gall bladder, spleen and pancreas.

The corresponding emotion of this chakra is anger while the mental component is will. Spiritually the third chakra is about self-determination. Although, anger may not seem to fit in here, it is part of the developmental process toward self-determination. Anger separates and defines boundaries. Toddlers heading into the third year of their lives use anger to separate from others so they can begin to know themselves. The misnomer of the "terrible twos" is actually referring to the third year and third chakra development of will.

The solar plexus has a strong correlation with the third eye energy center. If the head is like a mainframe computer, then the solar plexus is like a networking computer. The statement "as above, so below" aptly describes the relationship between these two centers. Whereas the third eye is all about psychic perception, the solar plexus is about intuition. When there is anxiety in the mind, there will be a corresponding tightening in the stomach area created by anxiety as well. Anytime healing work is done on the head, it should be balanced with the solar plexus and vice versa.

I attribute the adrenal glands to this chakra as well, although biologically the adrenals are associated with the root chakra and its focus on survival. The fight or flight mechanism of adrenals helped ancient humans determine whether to stay in the vicinity of mortal danger or to run. Modern humans use the adrenal glands from a psychological perspective. As the solar plexus is a mini-mind, it may interpret a mental stressor with great alarm sending a message to the root chakra to activate the adrenals. The modern mind is also not above just wanting the extra boost of adrenaline for the kick it provides, as it rarely wants to slow down or rest.

A serious physical ailment that creates problems at the mental level is adrenal exhaustion. Caused by the fight or flight mechanism switching on and not turning off while under chronic stress, the adrenals eventually become exhausted. Once this occurs, they are very hard to regenerate. The thyroid can then crash, along with the rest of the endocrine system, as it tries to take on the job description of the adrenals. In an extreme stage, adrenal exhaustion can bring about mental breakdown as we can no longer think clearly or perceive what is helping us and what is not. Alcoholism, drug addiction, agoraphobia, and suicide can be symptoms of extreme adrenal exhaustion. Elvis Presley, Marilyn Monroe and Howard Hughes all exhibited these forms of advanced and extreme exhaustion.

The solar plexus is the digestive center of the body. We digest energetically as well as physically. Similar to the brain's sensory integration mechanisms, the small intestines, in the solar plexus chakra, assimilates energy. When the small intestines cannot energetically process the information the body has ingested, we can experience physical constipation, emotional stagnation, and mental fogginess. Temper tantrums in children, or sudden, violent outbursts are the solar plexus blowing out energy that has become too overwhelming to integrate.

The solar plexus is often a crucial crossroads for people. As we receive the energy of our soul through the upper chakras, we also receive our spiritual gifts. These are the Divine gifts that each one of us brings to the planet. Indigenous people call it our "original medicine." If we do not feel worthy on a personal level, the solar plexus will not let this energy move all the way down to the root chakra. The spiritual gifts are then given out from the heart benefiting everyone else but ourselves. That's not what the Divine Creator intended! We must receive our own gifts first, embodying them at the solar plexus level, co-creating with them at the second chakra, and anchoring them into the Earth at the root chakra.

° **Heart Chakra** (*Fourth; Love*): The heart chakra lies between the lower three chakras and their connection with personality and the upper three that identify more with soul. As we spiritually evolve, the lines of demarcation between personality and soul soften and the chakras begin to carry a more unified energy throughout all of them. Traditionally the color associated with this chakra is green, but rose and gold are also associated with the heart. The hands, physical heart, lower lungs, thymus gland and the protective lining of the heart, called the pericardium, are all part of this chakra.

The heart is all about feeling. The emotional component of the heart chakra is love, while the spiritual component is compassion. Similar to the second chakra there is no mental quality. In an unbalanced state, we either don't own what the heart feels or conversely feel so much for another that we are incapable of living our own lives. In the first case, our heart chakra is closed down and we primarily come from the judgmental mind when relating to others. In the second case, our heart chakra is too open and merging so completely with another's suffering we bring our entire organism to a complete stop. Although we do not need to take on the suffering of others, our hearts may bear witness to suffering at a physical level while acknowledging the power of the soul to transcend all suffering.

A deep lying fear in many of us is the fear of our heart breaking. Pema Chodrun, a Buddhist nun, makes the claim in her book *The Wisdom Of No Escape: On The Path Of Loving Kindness*, that the heart is infinitely stronger than many of us realize. She describes a meditation practice called "tonglen"—inhaling that which is bothering us or affecting us negatively on a personal level, and exhaling the positive quality we want to replace it with. At some point we, as meditators, switch our perception from personal to global, and we inhale what is bothering us as a universal condition that many have experienced and exhale again that quality that replaces what's asking to be shifted or healed. This mediation practice shifts the paradigm that our hearts aren't strong or courageous.

In a meditation that I developed, called the *Four-Chambered Heart Meditation*, I address the four qualities of the heart, each one related to a heart chamber. These qualities are commitment, asking that each of us discover what our most sacred commitment is; constancy, the ability to stay the course in difficult times; clarity, the quality of a clear emotional body, and courage, the ability to face the tougher aspects of being a human. When these four qualities are balanced and stabilized then our entire emotional anatomy is strong and we stay physically strong in adverse times.

The heart in a balanced, loving state is the connected heart. Laughter is a physical expression of love and the heart loves a good belly laugh. When the heart opens fully to its awakened state, then its power is felt, seen and heard.

° **Throat Chakra** (*Fifth; Expression*): The throat is an important center. It is the bridge between the mind and the heart. The throat chakra contains the temporal bones, thyroid and parathyroid glands, the ears, larynx, and upper lungs. This is the seat of clairaudience, the ability to hear multi-dimensionally. If the thyroid glands are calibrated or aligned to higher dimension beings, we can channel their information through the throat. This chakra is associated with blue, the color of seeking inner truth. The emotional component is grief, the mental component is integrity, and the spiritual component is sacred sound. The throat loves toning and singing.

The throat is the center of speech and listening. Listening is a unique part of hearing. It is connected with will from the third eye center as we decide what we want to hear and what we don't. We connect energetically to people through listening and hearing. Linked with the middle ear, healthy listening will actually close the ear when receiving too much sound or open the ear when wanting to hear better. Trauma can affect listening by locking the ear in either a closed or open position. In the first case we don't receive enough sound to stimulate the brain and we begin to experience apathy and withdrawal. With the ear too open we are bombarded by sound, causing hyperactivity in children and usually an aversion to social gatherings. The ear also listens internally as the vagus nerve, which innervates the ear connects to every organ in the body. In dreams, as well as clairaudience, we can begin accessing information from our interior wellbeing. The temporal bones play an important part in the throat center's ability to listen. If out of balance, they cause vertigo and dizziness. The act of yanking on a person's ear, such as old school teachers used to punish children, can unbalance the temporal bones.

With speech our tasks are to use our voice effectively, speaking our truth without judgment and projecting our voice (throat linked with solar plexus) so that we may be heard.

In the first four chakras, the root and solar plexus chakras are primarily masculine, dynamic centers, while the sexual and heart chakras are feminine, receptive centers. The throat center holds both masculine and feminine as well as dynamic and receptive energies. Here our task is to master the balance of opposites and illusion of duality. Two such seeming opposites are giving and receiving. To be able to receive well is a gift to the giver. Giving can only be authentic if we've already received the same quality ourselves.

° **Third Eye Chakra** (*Sixth; Wisdom*): As the seat of clairvoyance the third eye is famous for its psychic abilities. It is associated with indigo, the color of the deep level of consciousness reached when meditating. It is located in the center of the forehead and the back of the head, at the base of the skull, and links with the brain, the sphenoid, pineal gland and thought. The emotional component of this chakra is bliss. Its mental component is discernment and its spiritual component is free will and choice. The ability to see auras lies within the third eye's heightened psychic or clairvoyance perception.

Humans tend to place a lot of importance on those who are clairvoyant. Like all spiritual gifts, clairvoyance, which is the ability to see multi-dimensionally, has a certain level of responsibility that comes with it. Clairvoyance and clairaudience must come through our belief systems held within the mind. If the personality/ego hasn't developed in a healthy and balanced way, then we can develop distorted belief systems that can cause poor interpretation of clairvoyant information. When listening to clairvoyant information from someone else, allow your body to help discern if the information is truthful for you. If the body resonates, expands or lifts then the information is of positive value to you. If it contracts or does nothing, then the information is not appropriate for you.

If we become mentally fixated or emotionally attached to a certain outcome or form in the future, we become off-centered as the mind moves into the energy fields in front of us. We risk using our will, a form of mental energy, to force a desired outcome. It's possible to get things done this way, but it creates karma as well as uses deep levels of core energy that over time become depleted. It also takes us out of universal timing and synchronicity.

Besides love, spiritual free will and choice is one of the greatest qualities that we have on Earth. It comes with tremendous responsibility but it also creates ultimate freedom. By developing discernment, we can begin to clarify what is right and appropriate for us. People who brainwash others, override free will and choice by sending their psychic energy through a person's third eye to break his will. Cults, political regimes, abusive spouses and even unethical collective agencies all use this tactic in hopes of gaining control over other people mentally, emotionally and physically. This also occurs spiritually in the form of energetic implants from wizard souls. The payoff is control of the unused or untapped power of the soul. Reiki never overrides another's free will and choice but honors the empowerment of this quality.

The pineal gland in the third eye is extremely potent. When it is infused with spiritual energy it "lights" up from within. This phenomenon often accompanies enlightenment. I have experienced this in the middle of the night when my whole head lit up inside. I thought someone had turned on the lights of the room but when I opened my eyes it was pitch black. Upon closing my eyes again, the inside room of my head was fully illuminated. The pineal gland can be calibrated to the Higher Self to access the spiritual wisdom contained in this level of the soul.

The sphenoid bone is an important component to the quality and ability to perceive in the third eye. This pivotal bone is located near the center of the head and articulates with almost every other bone in the cranium. Energetically it is a visionary bone. When the sphenoid is healthy we dream and vision with clarity, perception and revelation. When impacted or out of balance the sphenoid can create dyslexia, headaches and migraines, spinal scoliosis, personality change, eye dysfunction, manic depression, and morbid thoughts or suicidal tendencies.

When I first experienced Reiki, I had a particular kind of headache that comes from the sphenoid being out of rhythm with the occipital bone. It was a recurrent theme in my life, created from many head traumas and one that was only temporarily relieved with craniosacral therapy. In my Reiki session I felt my sphenoid self-correct and it never went out of balance again.

° **Crown Chakra** (*Seventh; Unity*): Just above the crown of the head, the seventh chakra is associated with purple or white light. It has the least interest in the needs of personality and every day concerns of materialism and time as it opens to the universal quality of oneness with the Divine. The crown chakra is linked with the upper part of the brain, the parietals and the pituitary gland. It has no emotional or mental component.

A crown chakra that is too open can overwhelm the other levels of chakras and bodies as too much spiritual energy enters the system. With a crown chakra too open we experience extreme spaciness, finding it hard to focus or concentrate. The more the upper three chakras open, the more balanced and grounded the lower three chakras should be. Reiki focuses on balancing all of the charkas.

Traditionally the pituitary gland is linked with the third eye and the pineal gland with the crown chakra. Energetically, though, I have found that the pituitary aligns or calibrates to the soul's point of origin through the crown chakra. This is the primary identity or place of belonging that the soul is linked to. It is the planet or galaxy from which we came before we took on Mission Earth. Our pituitary gland, like all glands, is a radio receiver, and once aligned to our point of origin begins to download information from our home place. This creates a sense of homecoming for the soul within the body after being adrift and alone from all that is familiar.

Vertical/Horizontal Energies

There are many energies running within us in all directions. Categorizing some of them vertically and horizontally is one way to check certain relationships within the body. Generally, **Vertical Energies** connect us to the Earth, our soul and multidimensional realms. Horizontal energies are what we use for connecting with human beings, organizations and other structures we create in our life. Optimally with balanced vertical and horizontal energies we are spiritually and humanly connected at the same time.

Within vertical energies is the **spiritual alignment**, containing the core column of light, our core essence, the grounding cord and hara line. Our spiritual alignment aligns us to our spiritual gifts, soul tasks and purpose. Soul tasks are those lessons and healings we need to master before we can open to our soul purpose, the ultimate gift we bring to the planet.

Children are part of their parents' spiritual alignments until they are age 12. At that time, they move into their own spiritual alignment and take on their individual karma and soul tasks. If there is a developmental delay and a child doesn't move into her spiritual alignment, it can create problems around becoming independent or discovering her unique self.

I have worked on adults who were still linked into a parent's spiritual alignment and working on that parent's soul tasks instead of their own. Joey was an 18-year old senior who was having a hard time in the last semester of her senior year. Mentally she was preparing for college, but emotionally she was struggling with the timing of moving out and becoming more independent from her family. It became harder and harder for her to concentrate and focus on her studies. She also felt tired all the time. Her sense of herself was that she was very creative but also business minded as well. When I read her energy fields I saw that she had disconnected from her mother's spiritual alignment at age 14, but hadn't yet disconnected from her father's spiritual alignment. Her father was a businessman who was very driven with his work. Because Joey hadn't disconnected from her father yet, she felt his "business" mind as her own. Although Joey had a strong mental field, her personal soul task and purpose was about expressing her heart energy in some form. Once she disconnected from her father's spiritual alignment, she was able to become more in sync with her own softer heart energy and honor her path of working with children in some capacity. This freed up her vital life force energy and she could once again concentrate and focus on her work while enjoying her life as well.

The **grounding cord,** containing the root chakra and the energy of the legs and feet, connects us physically with the Earth. It runs through all the physical chakras. Prior to birth we connect to the Earth through our Mother's umbilical cord. After birth this energetic cord should disconnect and we ground to the Earth through our own field. Again for various reasons we can avoid standing in our own power and chose to ground through other people's grounding cords. By strengthening the solar plexus and our sense of self-worth, we can hold a greater sense of empowerment in our stance on the planet. When we ground it should be to the center of the Earth. Then no matter where we are, we still have the same reference point of grounding.

The **hara line** is an energetic line that runs to the center of the Earth and up through our crown chakra to our connection with the Divine. It is associated with the emotional body. If the grounding cord helps orient our physical body to the planet, the hara line helps anchor the soul into this incarnation via the emotional body. Certain energy centers on the hara line are of great significance. The thymus gland located mid-sternum is a hara line center called "the seat of the soul's longing." It holds the information of our soul purpose. Below the navel is the hara point referred to in Chi Kung as the lower tan tien. This important point is where the soul enters the physical body when we are in utero, fusing with nature. Again, due to trauma or being out of sync with our development this can be delayed. In Chapter 7 there is an advanced technique that fuses soul with nature at this point. At the perineum is a hara line center that helps us transcend the physical, while behind the knees are two important centers that help align us to our soul's path.

When our emotional body is aligned in a healthy way with our Soul, we are then able to take care of our own emotional needs. If we love, honor, and respect ourselves, then we manifest loving, honoring and respectful relationships. If our emotional body is calibrated to our personality, we then become dependent on others to fulfill our emotional needs. Energetically this can show up as the hara line leaving the body at the navel and becoming an emotional umbilical cord into others. Conversely, a person might allow someone to cord his hara line into her. In the first case one feels unable to stand on her own, develops codependent relationships and exhibits extreme neediness that never seems to fill her up. In the latter scenario, a person might develop resentment toward those who are draining her and try to push them away. Similar to the grounding cord, the hara line can be realigned through our own energy fields to the center of the Earth.

Horizontal Energies are energy fibers that extend out in front, side and behind us. They also include our chakras as these energy centers have both vertical and horizontal energies. When we establish a sense of belonging through our root chakra and crown chakra then our horizontal energies allow us to connect in healthy ways. In relationships, energy fields overlap and create a third entity. Optimally in a relationship, we each stand empowered in our own vertical alignment, responsible for our own needs, and then expand horizontally in wholeness and connectedness, enhancing the other person's empowerment while receiving support from that person. If we collapse into the relationship entity, hoping that it will do for us what we aren't willing to do for ourselves, we create fractured relationships that are disempowered and co-dependent.

Energy Streams

Energy streams are bands of information that affect us on many levels. There are ancestral energy streams from our mothers and fathers. There can be additional ones, if adopted. Sometimes there are energy streams from religious and cultural roots. There are energy streams from the past (that are not linked in with karma) as well as from our future. Specialized energy streams that link into each of the endocrine glands bring information from other dimensions. Optimally these energy streams are supporting us moving forward on our soul's path. If they are not, then it is possible to energetically clear them from negative vibrational patterns.

Other Energy Channels including the Microcosmic Orbit

The meridians are channels that allow energy to flow through the body. You can run Reiki through the meridians to help open and clear them of blocks. I don't cover the meridians in this book but recommend that you find a book that lists them such as *Energy Medicine* by Donna Eden.

One important aspect created by two meridians is called the **Microcosmic Orbit**. This is referred to in the attunements. The Microcosmic Orbit is created when an energy line running down the front of the body, called the Conception Vessel, connects at the root chakra with the energy line running up the back of the body called the Governor Meridian. These two lines also connect at the head when the tip of the tongue is placed behind the front teeth making a continuous circuit of energy in the body. Connecting the Microcosmic Orbit is used in traditional and New Earth Reiki attunements.

Whew! You made it through this big topic. One final note: Don't worry about memorizing all of this information. It was meant to be and introduction to you and to prime your intuition. In the next chapter we'll explore how to tap into your intuition with muscle testing.

Chapter Four

Intuitive Communication

"The individual mind is like a computer terminal connected to a giant database. The unlimited information contained in the database has now been shown to be readily available to anyone in a few seconds, at any time and in any place."
-David R. Hawkins

Becoming attuned to New Earth Reiki, then using it, increases your energetic vibration. You become more intuitive, psychic, clairaudient and clairsentient, allowing you access to other realms for information and guidance. These gifts of psychic awareness are the natural consequence of spiritual growth or expansion and require new levels of understanding, responsibility and integrity to use them properly. It's a process I call "becoming intuitive with your intuition." Because all intuitive or psychic information comes through the filter of our belief systems, it's important to use discernment when interpreting this information.

One question that arises with increased intuition is whether we are receiving intuitive guidance about someone else or are we just perceiving our own energy mirrored back to us? In this chapter you'll be introduced to muscle testing, a valuable tool for checking or validating our intuition. Muscle testing taps into the wisdom of the body, circumnavigating the mind. Reading energy is often a challenge for the conscious mind because the world of energy often looks very different from form. The body, however, has access to wisdom that surpasses time and space constraints that the mind grapples with. Muscle testing, or kinesiology as it is also known, taps into this wisdom through yes or no questions. The underlying foundation for muscle testing is that a truth strengthens or enhances life, while a falsehood weakens us.

Muscle testing is an incredibly valuable tool to learn. It can be used to determine if a particular part of our energetic anatomy needs help or attention. It can also determine where the cause of a problem is located when all we can observe is an effect or a symptom. Muscle testing can verify intuitive information that we receive and, if we are helping another person, whether we should openly share that information with him. It can determine if a person is speaking from body attitude or ego or if she is speaking from core essence.

When people first learn muscle testing, they think the challenge is learning the form. Can they do it? Will they be able to discern yes/no answers? Learning a muscle testing form is simple and easy. In this chapter, I offer you different ways to muscle test, from two-handed to one-handed variations, or using a tool such as a pendulum. After choosing one that you resonate to, you'll want to practice, practice, practice. Give yourself permission to be incorrect so you can get beyond doubt. If you will consistently use muscle testing over a period of time, you will get very good at it. At that point a curious thing happens–you notice how you are asking the questions. Then the true art of muscle testing begins to make itself known.

Muscle Testing Tips

- **Clarify your intention.** Some people have trouble distinguishing the yes and no answers. Sometimes the clarity will be there and then fade. A simple solution to this difficulty is to relax internally, let go of wanting a certain response and then ask that the yes and no answers be more clear. Assert your genuine willingness to perceive and ask that the communication be made stronger and more distinct. Usually that will immediately improve the clarity. The energetic stance changes from pushing for an answer to letting an answer come to you.
- **Check your body**. Sometimes we simply become fatigued, dehydrated, or otherwise enough out of balance to distort the needed clarity of reception. Try drinking a glass of water or resting. Continue muscle testing when your focus has returned.

- **Calibrate your listening to your core essence.** With muscle testing, the most vital element is the willingness to actually perceive the information. Superimposing personal assumptions will completely distort the process and must be avoided. What is being practiced is the willingness to hear what is not known or expected. The left brain, in particular, thinks it knows the answer before it asks the question. Beware of the left brain asking the question in a way that is similar to "leading a witness." Ask your Energy Body to calibrate your listening to your core essence. This helps shift from ego to spiritual self.
- **Practice, practice, practice.** Getting good with muscle testing in a healing session requires getting comfortable with it as a tool. Practice using muscle testing in all areas of your life. Start where you don't have a great deal of emotional attachment (pizza versus is it cancer).
- **Release preparation techniques.** After the initial steps of learning a method, you no longer need to ask to be shown yes or no. Just simply do your chosen method whenever you ask a question.

Muscle Testing Methods

In the beginning to learn a method, set up your Crystalline Energy Fields with the Healing Chambers in the appropriate order for muscle testing. Try all the methods and notice which one you resonate to the most.

- **One-handed Method**

  This method actually tunes into the craniosacral rhythms of the body more than the muscular system. It works well for people who are very sensitive to their bodies.

1. Silently affirm your intention to communicate with the Energy Body.
2. Ask to connect to your kinesthetic sense. Bring your awareness into your nondominant hand.
3. Lightly touch together the pads of your index finger and thumb. Keep your hand and fingers relaxed.

4. Ask your fingers to show you "yes." (You'll feel a slight sensation between the two fingers as though a magnet were drawing them together.) Listen or feel for this, versus trying to "see" it.
5. Ask to be shown "no." (You won't feel anything between the two fingers, even though they are touching.)
6. Continue to practice asking yes/no questions throughout the day. Start with small things that don't feel emotionally charged. Be open to the answer even when your left brain can't explain it.
7. If you are working with another person and asking questions for her, you can lightly place your dominant hand on the person to establish a strong energetic connection.

- **Standing Method (no hands)**

1. Stand with knees slightly flexed.
2. Ask your body to show you "yes." Your body will sway slightly one way or another.
3. Ask your body to show you "no." Your body will sway a different way or not at all.
4. After understanding your method of yes/no, you don't need to ask again.
5. Once comfortable getting yes/no answers standing, try getting results in a sitting position.

- **Sticky Fingers (one hand)**

1. Place the middle finger of your nondominant hand on top of the index finger. Ask to be shown yes, then flick the middle finger off. It will feel sticky or resistant.
2. Replace the middle finger on the index finger. Ask to be shown no, then flick the finger off. It will have little resistance or not feel sticky.

- **Two-handed**

1. Bring your awareness into your hands.
2. Form two intertwined circles with thumb and index fingers.

3. Ask your fingers to show you yes. Quickly pull your dominant hand away from the nondominant hand. They will not easily break apart.
4. Reconnect your finger circles. Ask your fingers to show you no. Quickly pull your dominant hand away from the nondominant hand. They will easily break apart.

- **Pendulum**

1. Hold a pendulum (any weighted object on a string or chain) in your dominant hand. Keep your hand relaxed. Don't squeeze or pinch the pendulum.
2. Ask the pendulum to show you yes. It will move in a certain direction.
3. Ask the pendulum to show you no. It will move in a different direction.

The Art of Asking Questions

Once you begin to get comfortable with a method, start observing how your mind is asking the questions. In the beginning, you can get dizzy asking about anything and everything. Ultimately, though, ask when you are ready to receive information and work with it. If you've already made up your mind about what you are going to do, proceed with that plan. Getting confused or creating a conflict within yourself does not help with forward movement and growth.

One of the most important ways you can use muscle testing is for timing. In this manual, you have the opportunity to receive three levels of attunements. Through muscle testing you can determine the correct timing between these attunements so that your body, in particular the nervous system, has time to fully assimilate the energetic changes that occur. You can also muscle test for right timing between Reiki sessions.

Another factor in the art of asking questions is where you start the question process which is about checking your assumptions. When you need to check your assumptions, often the muscle testing is neither a clear yes nor clear no. For example: you decide to go out for the evening. You ask if the movies would be a good choice and your muscle testing is not a strong yes nor a strong no. So you ask if going to a coffee bar where a folk band is playing is a good choice. Again you get neither a clear yes nor a clear no. At this point you need to back up and begin to check whether or not going out is the appropriate thing to do. You might get a no, yet feel as though there is still a missing element. Suddenly it occurs to you to ask if you should invite someone over to watch movies with you at home. Eureka! Clear and strong yes.

Sometimes you can get different answers to the same question. What is going on here? If you ask from a level of survival you may get one response, while if you ask from a level of thriving you may get another. Remember, it's information that you are receiving. If some part of you goes into resistance with the answer, sit with the information for a while and ask your Energy Body to come up with a resolution. In a few days, approach the information again and see if there has been a shift around it.

Pay attention to your languaging in your questions. Our left brains are used to talking in short hand. When we get information through the body by muscle testing, language needs to be very literal. Questions need to be in such a form that they can be answered with a simple yes or no. That means asking one thing at a time.

Communicating with Guides

One of the great joys of Reiki is the opening of your awareness to Light Beings in other dimensions. Through the Crystalline Energy Field, you can connect to Ascended Masters, Nature Spirits, Reiki Guides or Guardians as well as your Higher Self. Information can come from a "collective" (all your guides) in one voice or from a particular guide using muscle testing and your intent to connect to that guide. The more you do this, the more your other senses begin to open, including your ears to clairaudience.

For some people it is important that they know their personal Spirit Guides. These are guides who are with you throughout your life. Usually people have 4-6 Spirit Guides (you can muscle test how many you have). One comes in at birth, then usually one around age 4-6, then 8-10, and a fourth one around 12-14. A fifth guide can show up sometime between 16-20. These types of Spirit Guides have incarnated before so they understand the experience of a soul in a human experience. They are not your deceased family members or animal companions.

Ask to connect to them through the Crystalline Energy Field, even if you don't know them by name. Begin muscle testing to converse with them. You can enhance the communication by asking that your ears calibrate to their vibration. If you think you just heard something from them but aren't sure if it was your guides or your own thoughts, muscle test to validate what you are perceiving.

In the Advanced Reiki Training, we work more with the Spirit Guides, determining whether any are "negative," need to be updated or if you have another one waiting to connect with you. Negative, by the way, is referring to a type of guide that we called in because of certain negative circumstances in our life that we felt unable to cope with. It's important to release them in appreciation and gratitude when they are no longer needed.

Becoming an Energy Reading Master

We all read energy. Our bodies and energy fields are constantly scanning and reading different energetic vibrations from our environment. This information comes in through the subconscious or manifests as body symptoms, which become conscious to us after the energetic information is interpreted through the belief systems and perceptions held in the brain's interpretation centers. To become a master energy reader takes much practice and a willingness to let go of misperceptions that have developed from your experiences over time. For example, if as a child you were bit by a dog, you might form the belief system or perception that all dogs are aggressive and more apt to bite than not. Using Reiki as a healing tool, you can heal those types of wounds and release the belief systems that have linked to the original trauma and are now currently limiting you.

As you continue to use Reiki, your higher sense perceptions open up, becoming even more heightened to subtle energies. You receive multidimensional information kinesthetically through the body, auditorially, visually or through smelling. In healing sessions, I have suddenly smelled cedar, sweet grass, coffee and other smells. Then my discerning brain must decide what information the smell represents. Is it coming from the person's physical body indicating a need to release toxins? Or is it coming from a guide who is announcing himself through the smell of coffee? If I have a belief system that coffee is bad for the health, I might jump to the conclusion that the person on the table needs to quit drinking coffee. Before I make that statement to the receiver, however, I muscle test to get a better sense of my perception.

Receiving information kinesthetically or through your feeling senses can be especially difficult to interpret. Generally, when you feel something in your body, you identify with it as something going on within yourself. A form of this is empathic sensitivity when you feel other people's feelings. You can suddenly become depressed, fearful or angry without it relating to your own life. If you have a strong sense of yourself, it's easier to discern whether these feelings are yours or not. Muscle testing, however, helps with the discernment process.

We are constantly being affected by other's energies including thoughts. I have often wondered how many of my own thoughts are even mine. I suspect it's only about 20%. (I muscle tested the amount). We can pick up thoughts not only from an individual but also mass consciousness.

One indicator that what you are experiencing in your body is not your own is when the symptoms cannot be read by doctors or other health practitioners. If your body doesn't respond to certain medications (or energy healing), it can indicate that you are trying to treat someone else's symptoms in your own body.

Intuitive sensory overwhelm can be quite painful. I have several ways that I deal with this downside of my gifts. First, I make sure I have a strong energy field or aura. Doing the Tree Meditation (from the Advanced Reiki Training) helps with this. Then I reconnect to my Crystalline Reiki Symbol with both my 3 energy streams and my 5 Crystalline Energy Centers (explained in Chapter 5). I set up or reset my fields to keep my vibration high. I also get very aware of my boundaries, saying "no" to time wasters or those who don't respect my gifts. My final tool that I use in extreme cases is a protocol from Crystalline Consciousness Technique called *Expressing Your Purpose*. You can find out more about this protocol in the appendix.

With all my tools and awareness, it can still be difficult. When my sister died, for a while my grief appeared primarily in physical symptoms. I stayed present with the process allowing the energy of grief to move through me as needed. Then I went through a phase when my pancreas kept falling out of balance. This caused me to excessively crave sweets. However, nothing I ate seemed to alleviate the pancreas even for a short while. My brain interpreted the problem from an old story line of being an over eater. I was disheartened to think that with all my healing this old place had resurfaced during the emotional processing of my sister passing. I sent up a silent request to my guides to help me heal my pancreas.

That night I dreamed my daughter died. I went into her room and was devastated with grief that she had died. I was also aware of all of the grief of my family members about the passing of my daughter. In the dream I picked up a note written by my mother and it said, "Not her, oh God, not her."

I woke in tears and confusion. Was this dream about me? Was it about my daughter and something that might occur in the near future? I entered into a meditative state and began asking my guides for more information to better interpret the dream. From this place I was shown that the dream was not only information for me about my pancreas but it was also information for me about my mother. By experiencing the loss of a child in my dream, I understood that my body had been empathically experiencing the loss that my mother was feeling for her daughter. The grief I was feeling, was the grief that any mother feels for another mother who has lost a child.

Usually at this point in reading energy, my body will release the felt symptom giving me the indicator signal that I have totally received the information. In this case my pancreas continued to hurt and ache, but I no longer interpreted it to be about sweets. It was my signal that I was energetically supporting my mother in her own grief process for the loss of her child. I took a more proactive stance with this support and began to send Reiki to my mother and father every day to help them deal with their loss. My pancreas finally settled down.

Now it's time to become attuned to Reiki! In the next chapter we look at New Earth Reiki Level 1. You'll receive an activation and learn the symbol. Then practice, practice, practice on yourself for 3 weeks. Meanwhile, don't forget to set up your fields every day and keep practicing your muscle testing.

Chapter Five

New Earth Reiki 1

"We now recognize that human intelligence is composed of multiple potentials that must be intentionally ignited and activated." -Stephanie Pace Marshall

Initiations have been used throughout the history of many cultures and spiritual traditions to prepare and expand human consciousness. Whether that is a shamanic rite of passage for puberty or a spiritual initiation used by Taoists, the result is the same—access to new levels of spiritual abilities, information and power.

A Reiki attunement, or initiation, is a mystical experience filled with wonder and awe. In our society, such an experience is rarely available to anyone who has not spent years studying spiritual growth and expansion. Although each person receiving an attunement experiences something different, almost everyone senses the sacredness of what is happening.

The Reiki attunement opens energy channels in the body to the flow of Reiki energy. Traditionally a Reiki Master does this by increasing the amount of Chi held in his or her body, linking it to the Reiki symbols and intention and then with their breath, transfers this Chi to the recipient. In this form of initiation, the amount of power that a Reiki Master holds determines the level of empowerment of the attunement. This in turn dictates how powerful a practitioner is, at least initially, in his healing work.

In New Earth Reiki, the attunement uses the tools of Crystalline Consciousness Technique. This allows you to connect directly to Reiki and be attuned by the Reiki guides or guardians. Master Usui, the originator of Reiki, was attuned in this way.

New Earth Reiki Attunements

There are three levels of attunements, one each for a different level of Reiki. Traditionally there is a minimum of 2-3 months between levels one and two, and 4-6 months (or up to two years for some teachers) between levels two and three. New Earth Reiki has an accelerator factor that comes with the Crystalline Energy System. You can typically do them at one month intervals. Use your muscle testing to check your particular timing and trust the answer you get. Additionally, you can repeat the attunements periodically as they are healing in and of themselves.

New Earth Reiki Level I

This level of Reiki brings the newcomer into the energy field of Reiki, opening energetic channels in the body to the flow of Reiki. During the attunement, you'll receive a symbol that you will start to work with. Called Cho Ku Rei (choe koo ray), this symbol "turns on" the flow of Reiki when you begin to work, essentially acting like an amplifier. The physical body particularly likes this symbol. Spend some time each day with this symbol so that it becomes embodied before preceding to the next level of Reiki.

In the beginning of the Reiki I attunement, you'll connect to your New Earth Reiki Symbol and then your fields will be set up for you. You'll be prepared energetically for the attunement with the first two phases of Crystalline Consciousness Technique. At the point of intention, you'll connect to the Reiki Guardians. These Light Beings of great power can be found at the further most edges of your light body and are responsible for bringing Reiki to the planet. They are also responsible for the evolution of Reiki as the planet's energy continues to increase. They are not to be confused with Reiki Guides, who are closer to our physical reality. Reiki Guides can be people you knew who have transitioned or who were with you if you used Reiki in other lifetimes. Reiki guides can also be pets who have transitioned and continue to participate with you in your healing work. Your personal Spirit Guides may show up as well.

After connecting to the Reiki Guardians, you'll state your intent to receive a first level New Earth Reiki Attunement.

Next an intent to connect the Microcosmic Orbit and Hara Line is spoken. With each intentional statement, there is a pause while the energy moves through your body.

New Earth Reiki is brought into your body at two points: Center Above and Center Below. These are two chakras that are located about 12 inches above the Crown Chakra and below the feet. The Reiki Symbol, Cho Ku Rei, is anchored into the hands, third eye and Hara Line.

Also during this attunement process, the Reiki Principles are anchored into your heart. These five principles are part of the traditional Reiki training that all practitioners and Reiki Masters aspire to live by. To have them anchored into your heart is an amazing experience.

After you experience your attunement, stay quiet for a while longer to allow your body to completely assimilate all of the energy.

After the attunement, you will want to give yourself healing treatments to help establish the flow of Reiki through your hands and to smooth out the increase of energy running through your system.

Do this once or twice daily, if possible, for 21 days following an attunement. Also embody the symbol and the 5 Reiki principles (check out the healing meditation for this later in this chapter). At this level just focus on working on yourself. In the next level you'll begin working on others.

Please listen to the New Earth Reiki I attunement now.

Reiki Symbol and How to Use It

Learn the symbol by drawing it in the air or on paper and saying its name three times. When using it in a healing session draw it in the palm of your hands while saying its name three times, then tap your palm or clap your hands together softly (three times).

Cho Ku Rei

The Connector

Element: Earth

Pronounced: *Choe Koo* ***Ray***

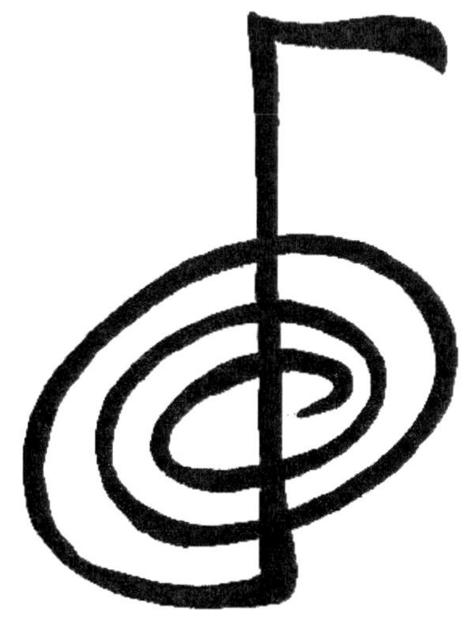

Cho-Ku-Rei

Cho Ku Rei is a beautiful symbol that can be used to consciously connect you to the Reiki energy at the beginning of each session. It has a warm, vital, loving feel to it. It says "Remember who you are." Traditionally it is considered the symbol for physical body healing. It helps to remove energetic blocks in the body so that all energies flow through the body more evenly. It also brings into the conscious mind the unconscious attitudes, feelings or beliefs that are affecting us in a subtle way.

Some suggestions for its use are:

- Draw it clockwise for increasing energy, counter-clockwise for decreasing.
- Increase positive qualities in a home or office by beaming it with the palms of your hands into a room or imagine drawing it on all four walls, ceiling and floor.
- Amplify nutritional value of food by drawing and invoking it over the food.
- Program a crystal for a specific purpose. Clarify your intention for the crystal, then invoke Cho Ku Rei and link it to the intention. Place your hands on the crystal and let Cho Ku Rei carry the intention into the crystal.

- Amplify positive effect of medicine. Invoke Cho Ku Rei and hold the medicine as you let the symbol flow into the medicine.

Embodied Reiki Symbol Meditation

Use this meditation to embody and activate your own conscious and energetic connections with the symbols. After this meditation you'll have a more innate sense about when and where to use the symbols. Essentially they'll begin to create with you as they speak through your consciousness. After each level, return to this meditation and embody the new symbols with it. Typically, once is enough when doing this meditation, but if you found yourself forgetting the symbols, do it several times.

1. Connect to your New Earth Reiki Symbol.
2. Set up your individual and crystalline group fields. Place the healing chambers in the appropriate order for embodying the Reiki Symbol(s).
3. Ask to connect to the Crystalline Grids of the planet and the Crystalline Energy Field.
4. Invoke Cho Ku Rei (say it three times and draw it in the air). Picture it above the crown of your head. With your intent, see, perceive or imagine the symbol coming into the crown, slowly moving down through your head, throat, chest, stomach and then into the small intestines. Here you will embody this symbol. Observe what shifts and changes for you. When the energy completes shifting, move to the next step.
5. State the Reiki Principles with both hands on your chest. Invite them to become embodied within you.

Reiki Principles

Just for today I will give thanks for my many blessings.

Just for today I will not worry.

Just for today I will not be angry.

Just for today I will do my work with integrity.

Just for today I will be kind to myself and every living thing.

Self-Healing Session

To do a self-healing session with the traditional chakras you'll start from top and move down. Invoke Cho Ku Rei in your hands then hold the hand position and wait for an indicator signal such as a sigh or shift in your body or awareness before moving on. You can also muscle test, if you're not sure of the timing.

Note: Working on yourself is one of the toughest things to do because we are taught to care for others but not for ourselves. Make it part of your yoga, meditation or bath routine so it becomes second nature. After each attunement, do self-healing daily for 3 weeks.

- Crown Chakra: Place the palms of your hands on either side of your head above the ears. Let the fingers be open at the midline of the top of your head. Don't cover the crown chakra.
- Third Eye Chakra: Place one hand on your forehead and one on the back of the skull at the base (just above the neck).
- Throat Chakra: Place one hand on the front of your neck and one hand on the back.
- Heart Charka: Place both hands on your chest with fingers overlapping at the midline. An excellent position for falling asleep.
- Solar Plexus Chakra: Place both hand across your stomach, above the belly button.
- Sexual Creative Chakra: Place both hands above the pubic bone, but below the belly button.
- Base Chakra: Place both hands on the top of your thighs.

Root Chakra	Sacral Chakra	Solar Plexus	Heart Chakra	Throat Chakra	Third Eye	Crown Chakra
Basic Trust	Sexuality, Creativity		Love, Healing	Communication	Awareness	Spirituality

Chapter Six

New Earth Reiki II

"It is said that one mark of an advanced civilization lies in its ability to communicate vast amounts of information by encoding it in the shortest possible space, such as in an abstract symbol." -Freddy Silva

When you've been attuned to Reiki something wonderful happens. You begin to have Reiki energy flow through you at all times. The Reiki symbols then amplify and focus this energy from general to more specific. The primary four Reiki symbols (omitting Raku) relate to one of the four energy bodies–physical, emotional, mental and spiritual. Reiki symbols may be used intuitively or systematically, individually or in combinations. In New Earth Reiki Level II you'll receive another activation and work with two more symbols for the emotional and mental levels. At this level you'll also begin working on others.

Let's get started! Listen to the Attunement for New Earth Reiki II now. Don't forget to use the embodied symbol meditation from Chapter 5 and work on yourself for 3 weeks.

Level 2 Reiki Symbols and How to Use Them

Sei He Ki

The Aligner

Element: Water

Pronounced: *Say **Hay** Kee*

Sei He Ki is often associated with the emotional body and healing of the emotional component in traumas, illnesses or external events. If the emotional component isn't addressed, illness or chronic problems may clear up only to surface in a different form in our lives. In acute trauma the emotional state can slow down the recovery rate.

Sei He Ki has a strong quality of enlightened love about it. This is because it represents divine order held in the higher spiritual realms. To move into greater health and wholeness the body needs to establish greater coherency through all of its systems. The reverse of coherency is entropy or breaking down of the systems. Sei He Ki reestablishes divine order through what is in disorder in this dimension.

This symbol works with the water element of our body, that holds the resonance of the divine order. It aligns you to your soul's purpose and divine will. When you are in alignment with divine order you merge with and become divine love. Then the higher spiritual realm of emotions can blossom and you'll experience bliss, joy, peace and contentment.

Some of the ways to use Sei He Ki are:

- Align the conscious mind with subconscious mind so that they are working together and not in conflict. Place one hand on the forehead and one on the solar plexus, then invoke the symbol into both levels of consciousness.

- Use it for protection. Place it in front, back and sides of your car while driving or in the corners of your house.
- Purify and release negative energies in food, crystals, buildings, land, etc. Use Sei He Ki first to clear, then Cho Ku Rei to amplify positive energy of food or to program crystals with a specific purpose.
- Release attachments of negative energy entities. Visualize the symbol in ultra violet and place it around the area that holds the attachment.
- Clear medicines from harmful side effects with Sei He Ki, then amplify positive qualities with Cho Ku Rei.
- Paired and upside down this symbol balances the left/right brain hemisphere, often the source of migraines, nightmares or a sudden change in disposition.

Hon Sha Ze Sho Nen
Time Traveler

Element: Air

Pronounced: *Hawn Shaw **Say** Show Nen*

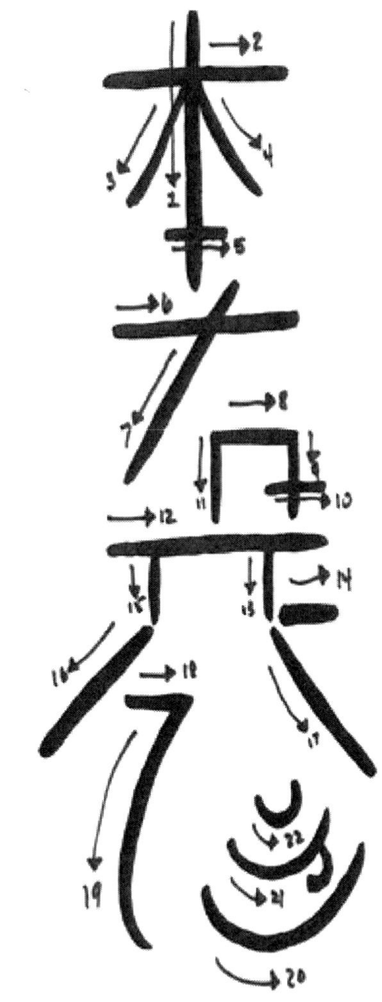

Hon-Sha-Ze-Sho-Nen

This "big" symbol is known as the distance symbol for sending Reiki to people not in the same room. It can also be used to time travel to heal past lives or events from earlier in one's life that still need healing. Because of its ability to surf time, it also helps to bring in Divine Timing. It's also intimately connected with the craniosacral system in the body, a system that synthesizes higher spiritual frequencies in the body during spiritual expansion. It represents Divine Mind or the ability of the One Source to consciously know itself.

Some of the ways you can use this symbol are:

- To do a long distance healing treatment set up fields from yourself individually and a group with the person who's going to receive Reiki. Invoke this symbol, then send all the symbols including Hon Sha again. Always ask for permission before doing a long distance treatment, either in person or to the Higher Self. If you don't get a strong yes, then don't persist.
- To release limiting belief systems, invoke Hon Sha then add the intention that it takes you to when the belief system first started (the original trauma). Use Sei He Ki to heal and clear the trauma.

- Heal negative karmic patterns in relationships. Invoke the symbol and use your intention to go "back" to when the karmic pattern first started. Use all of the symbols to heal this point in time.
- Invoke stillpoint. This is the temporary stopping of the craniosacral rhythm. This cessation of rhythm allows all levels and systems of the body to attain greater coherency and synchronization. Stillpoint can last for a few seconds or several minutes. The body knows how and when to start the rhythm again.
- Set up a repeating long distance treatment. Use the curly cue on the bottom portion of the symbol to establish how often and for how long your long distance healing treatment will be repeated. Especially useful in acute or emergency situations.
- When you feel you have moved to a new level of spiritual growth, use Hon Sha Ze Sho Nen to travel into the future and send all of the Reiki symbols to yourself to clear karma from the new level.
- Invoke right timing through all levels, components and systems of your being. Draw Hon Sha down the front of the body of a person you are working on or a picture of yourself.

Working on Others...Right Energetic Attitude

- Check your assumptions at the door about what is possible or what needs to happen.
- Always honor a person's innate wisdom about their timing of healing.
- Be careful of your languaging, which can unnecessarily limit another. Preface intuitive insights with "In my perception..." If a person asks for advice, make statements such as "If it were my problem or situation, I would..."
- Have the intention of connecting core essence to core essence.
- Let Reiki do the work.
- **The psychic energy of the mind is in an open, receptive state and becomes the observer. Do not send it into the client's body.** Reinforce this by reconnecting to your New Earth Reiki Symbol.

- Set up your individual crystalline and crystalline group field. Your crystalline group includes the person you'll be working on. Place the Healing Chambers in the appropriate order for the Reiki session.
- You have a unique signature in the way you get intuition. The challenge isn't to perceive the way someone else does, but to understand how you perceive. Begin to observe when you self-edit your perceptions. Develop your intuition about when to speak and when not to speak about your in-sights. Use your muscle testing!
- Observe how a person looks, feels, or sounds before and after working with them. If they aren't noticing any changes themselves, bring it to their attention.

Table Tips

- Use a massage table, if possible!
- Make sure your table is at the right height for you before your friend or family member arrives.
- Always bolster under the knees with a pillow and under the head or neck slightly with a towel or a soft pillow. If your massage table is hard, add a foam pad to it.
- Cover the person with a silk cover or warm blanket.
- Make sure your hands are clean and don't smell strongly of perfume or other smells.
- Watch your own body as you work. If you are tense or uncomfortable, you will transmit it to the recipient. If you get tired standing, try sitting down. If your arms are tired, find ways to prop them on the table (not on the receiver's body!).

Touch and Moving to a New Position

- Gently lift hands off the body. Don't drag or pull them through the energy field.
- Pay attention to how the body responds to your touch. Some bodies like firm touch, some like soft, some like none. Some are different in one part versus another.
- Drop your awareness into your hands and keep your hands relaxed.

- The indicator signal tells you when to move to the next hand position. Sometimes it comes from the person on the table. More often it is comes from yourself. Some people sigh. Some feel a change in the hands. When you get it right, the receiver might feel your hands are still in the same position even though you've moved. Don't be afraid to go back to a hand position, if you feel you moved too soon. You can also muscle test to determine if it's time to move.

Hand Positions

To do a session on someone in person, get them comfortable on the massage table. Invoke each of the symbols by drawing them in your hand and tapping the pams three times or clapping softly. Place your hands on the following hand positions and again invoke the symbols in your mind visually and saying its name three times.

A traditional Reiki session works primarily with the chakras. Don't feel limited by this. If you would like to place your hands somewhere else that needs Reiki, such as the knees, elbows or hands, by all means do so. The hand positions are: four head positions; neck; chest; solar plexus; low belly or sacrum area; and tops of the thighs or feet for the root chakra. The following photos show the positions from the front of the body. You can reach the back of the body in a couple of ways.

- Have someone turn over and work directly on their back.
- Send Reiki down the back when your hands are cradling the back of the head.
- Sandwich the torso by sliding one hand under the body with the other hand above. You can do this at the neck, heart, solar plexus and low belly. To easily slide your hand under someone, lift the sheet they are lying on, slightly lifting the person as well, and slide your hand underneath the sheet.

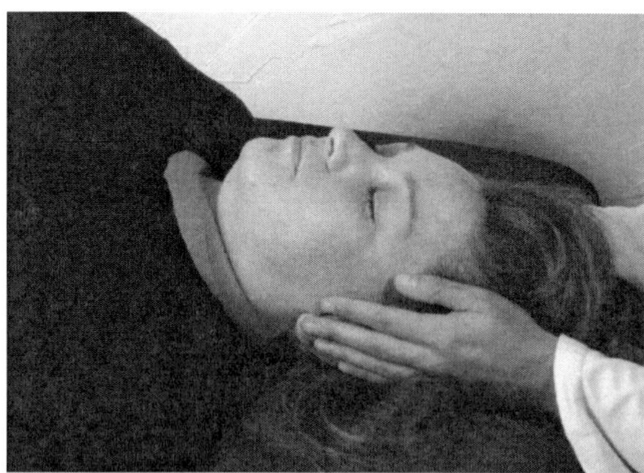

Hand Position #1: Place hands lightly along sides of head.

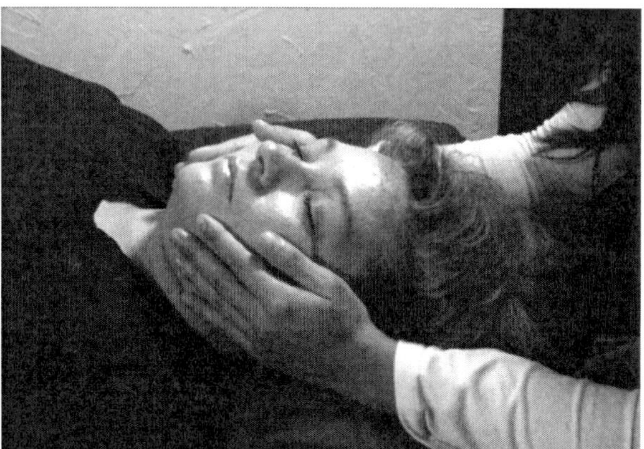

Hand Position #2: Place hands lightly alongside the jaws.

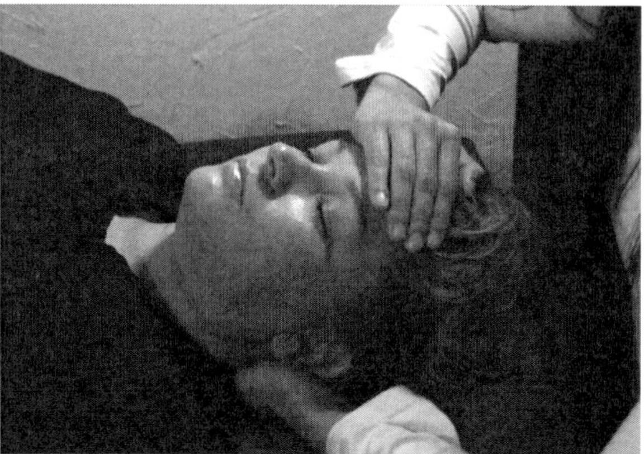

Hand Position #3: Place hands underneath back of head and lightly on forehead.

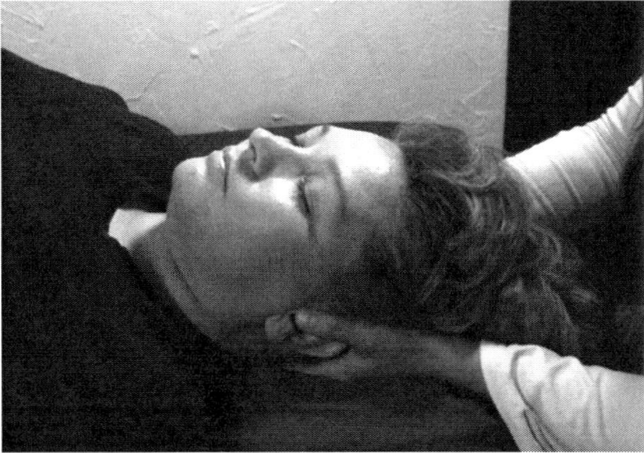

Hand Position # 4: Cradle back of head. Fingertips are down on the neck. Send Reiki energy down the back if you wish.

Hand Position #5: Neck. From the head of the table place one hand under the neck and one above. Check that the receiver feels comfortable and not feeling choked. Alternate position: Both hands above the neck, one on either side.

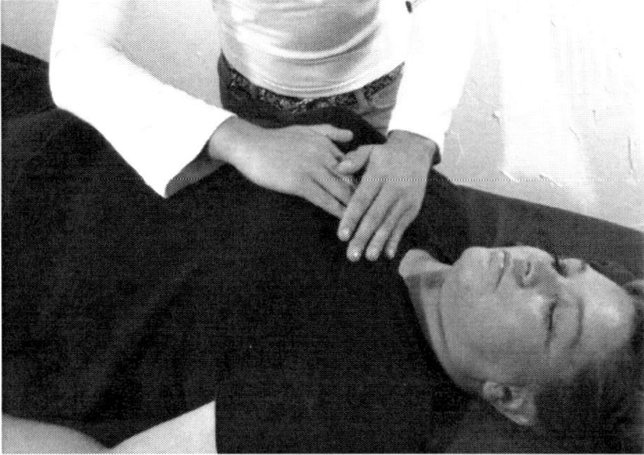

Hand Position #6. T position on chest. Alternatively place one hand underneath and one hand on top sandwiching the heart chakra. Ask permission to place hands directly on the chest area, in the front. If not sure, keep hands slightly off the body

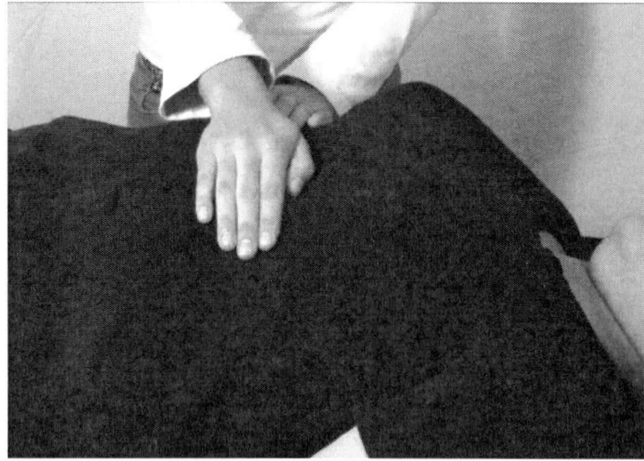

Hand Position #7. Solar plexus. Alternatively place one hand underneath the body while the other stays on top sandwiching the solar plexus.

Hand Position # 8: Second Chakra. Alternatively place one hand underneath the low back and the other above the pubic bone toward the head. Get permission from your receiver to place hand directly on the body. Otherwise leave the hand slightly off the body.

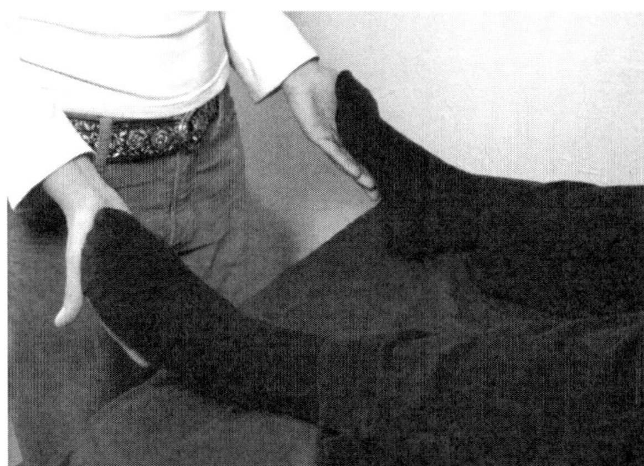

Hand Position #9: Either top or bottom of the feet for root chakra. You can also place your hands on the tops of the thighs just below the hip crease, as well as the feet.

Chapter Seven

New Earth Reiki III

"Breathing in, I am a mountain, imperturbably still, alive, rigorous. Breathing out, I feel solid, the waves of emotion can never carry me away." -Thich Nhat Hanh

In this chapter you'll receive the attunement for New Earth Reiki III and learn two new symbols and how to incorporate them in a session. You'll also learn energy healing principles, how to do a distance session and work on animals using New Earth Reiki.

As mentioned in the preface, the intention for this manual is to provide a personal healing tool for yourself, your friends and family. When we find a potent tool that we like, we can be overzealous in our presentation of this tool to family. This can create a problem for family or friends who might not quite share the same level of enthusiasm. Please honor your friends and family, without taking it personally, if they say "no" to a session with you. Share with them the results you are getting in your life with Reiki, let them know you are willing to work on them, and then let them ask you when they are ready. If your family is fairly conservative, keep your explanation of Reiki simple and to the point. Call it a form of "hands-on-healing" and point out how it can benefit them. Reiki is not a religion but it is spiritual.

Principles of Energy Healing

- I honor the Divine Wisdom inherent within everyone.
- To the best of my ability I will not project my own wounds on others.
- I am a channel for Universal Energy, not the originator of it.
- I never force my will on another—I seek always to empower.
- I release all expectations of what a "good" outcome is.
- I am a facilitator of healing, not someone's cure.
- I always honor free will and choice.
- Sometimes a negative is a positive.
- I will not offer advise contrary to a doctor's advice.
- I will not diagnose a medical condition.

The last principle about diagnosing or taking a medicine is something that people will ask you. If someone has been prescribed a medication that they don't want to take, they might ask you to confirm that they can stop taking it. Encourage them to return to their doctor to discuss their concerns. You may also intuit that someone you are working on has cancer or some other disease. Be very careful with your language about what you are perceiving. Legally, you cannot diagnose any illness. Before you scare the pants off of someone, you might also do a before and after comparison. Did whatever you were concerned about shift after a healing Reiki session? A good rule of thumb is to do three sessions or wait three weeks after a session to determine if you should recommend they see a doctor. When I was in India learning the Oneness Blessing and having physical symptoms appear after their attunements (a common sign of a healing crisis after transformation), I asked one of the dhasas (guides) about it and they didn't hesitate to say, "See a doctor." Not because it was serious, but because they absolutely wouldn't diagnose any physical symptoms. It was a good boundary to hold.

Let's get started with New Earth Reiki 3 now! Listen to the attunement then learn and memorize the symbols. Don't forget to embody the symbols in the meditation in Chapter 5 and do healing on yourself for three weeks.

Level 3 Reiki Symbols and How to Use Them

Dai Ko Myo

The Evolver

Element: Fire

Pronounced: *Die **Koe** Mee Oh*

This symbol holds both the Divine Masculine and the Divine Feminine facets of the Creator Source, as represented by the lightning bolt and the spiral. At the moment in time when the great void of pure potential receives the spark from Creator then form is conceived.

This symbol is associated with the spiritual body. Healing at this level is healing from the highest source or first cause. This symbol can also help you express the highest possible potential in any inherent form or structure. It evolves you consciously, spiritually, emotionally and physically.

Some of the ways you can use this symbol are:

- Heal genetic level problems. Connect to the organ or place that is malfunctioning and use Dai Ko Myo to "realign" the tissue to its genetic blue print.
- Begin any treatment with Dai Ko Myo so that the highest potential of any situation can be reached.
- Use it reversed to release negative energy. Visualize a large reversed Dai Ko Myo three feet beneath you or someone you are working with. State your intention to release all negative, stagnant, and other energies from your body. Visualize it traveling up through the body and aura to 6 feet or so above the head. At this point release any energies gathered by sending them on to their next level

of evolution. Reverse the symbol to its normal spiral and bring the symbol back down to three feet below the feet.

- Connect yourself to your higher purpose. Use Dai Ko Myo and your intention to connect, then double Cho Ku Rei's to ground this purpose in the physical.

Raku
The Unveiler

Element: Quintessence (all elements)

Pronounced: Raw **koo**

Raku is the one symbol that doesn't need to be invoked by calling its name three times. You can simply draw the symbol in the air and say Raku once to invoke it. Raku is used in traditional attunements to ground the Reiki energy as well as separate the auric fields of the Reiki Master and the receiver of the attunement. Additionally, it activates the Hara Line, helping the receiver bring the Reiki energy through his Ki channels and then grounds it in the Hara Center. Raku unveils and declares the truth in each situation.

Some of the other ways you can use Raku are:

- To separate. Stop psychic attacks or manipulation by drawing it between you and the incoming energy. It also cuts any energy cords or hooks that may have been place within you.
- Dislodge entrenched negative patterns by drawing it between you and the patterns not wanted.
- Use it to open portals of energy streams such as the ancestral energy stream. Once opened all Reiki symbols can be sent through to promote healing of the ancestral lineage. Other energy streams are from the past and into the future, spiritual lineage, cultural, racial, and religious.

- The fire serpent version of Raku can be used at the end or beginning of a healing session to align all the chakras and the energy bodies simultaneously allowing the Reiki energy to penetrate in a deeper manner. This is especially effective for people whose energy fields are fragmented from drug use, or people with connective tissue disorders.

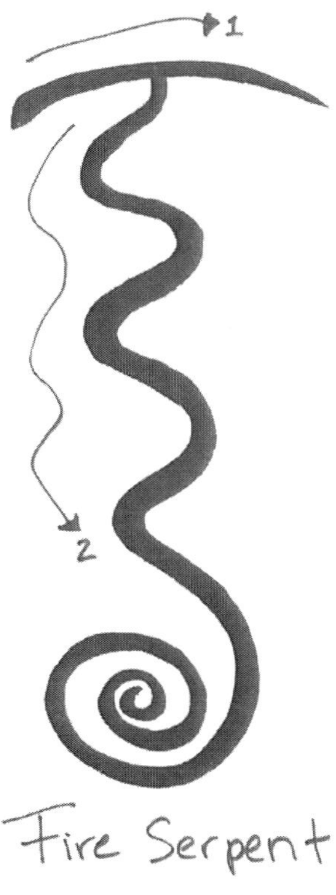

Protocol for a New Earth Reiki Session | Putting It All Together

Use this protocol as a starting place for creating your own unique session.

Before your receiver arrives:

- Connect to your New Earth Reiki Symbol with your 3 Primary Energies
- Set up your Individual Crystalline Energy Field and your Crystalline Group Field with the person you're going to work on. Place the healing chambers in the appropriate order for the New Earth Reiki session.
- Connect to the Crystalline Grids of the planet and the Crystalline Energy Field

After the receiver arrives

- Ask them what they are concerned about. Get info by observing the quality of their breathing, the light in their eyes, etc.
- Offer water (energy moves better if they're hydrated).
- If person is unfamiliar with a session, explain what is going to happen.

Receiver on table

- Use towel or pillow for head; pillow under knees.
- Invoke the 4 main symbols by saying their names three times while drawing them once in the palm of your hand and clapping or tapping hands softly three times.
- Place hands on a person's body and wait for the energy fields to connect with you.
- Silently or out loud state "The key to freedom is to be fully in the body."
- Keep hands soft, open and receiving.
- Work systematically through the chakras and hand positions as shown in Chapter 6 invoking the symbols intuitively, or invoking all of them at each hand position.

Finishing the Session

- Draw Fire Serpent over their head and down front of body
- Hold feet and invoke double Cho Ku Rei from hips to feet for grounding (see Chapter Five for this configuration)

- Let them know you're finished and then allow them time to slowly come out of the session
- Offer water, if they seem really spacey, or point fingertips at their feet to continue to help them ground
- Invite them to observe how they feel now about their body or whatever the situation was they were concerned with. Ask them to look in a mirror to see if they notice anything different about how they appear.

Doing a Distance Session

You can work with someone on the phone or with a photo of the person. You can also use a stuffed animal that represents who you are working on (please, please, please get their permission. The one exception is if it's a family member who cannot answer you if you ask because of a medical condition. Then ask their higher self). A fun thing to do with children is to do a session on a stuffed animal and them give it to them to sleep with at night.

- Start by connecting to your New Earth Reiki Symbol and setting up fields as described on page 78.
- Invoke all the symbols in the palms of your hands.
- Draw Hon Sha on the photo or the stuffed animal representing the person you are working on. If you are working with someone on the phone, draw a stick figure and draw the symbol on it.
- With someone on the phone, state where you are working (I'm now doing Reiki at your head) then silently invoke the symbols. Let Reiki stream from your hands toward the photo, stuffed animal or the person in your mind's eye.
- Use your muscle testing to determine when to move to the next hand position.
- If working with someone on the phone, check in and ask them how they are feeling when finished.

Note: Because of the ability of Reiki to "travel" from the hands, be careful how you place your hands in a photo. You can end up sending Reiki to whoever looks at the photo.

Working on Animals

Animals and children know you have healing energy to offer them and will generally hang out in your aura. They love it! You can easily work on animals by sending them all the symbols as you lay your hands on them. To start animal communication with them, ask questions then muscle test for the answers. Be open to what they are communicating, without projecting your own ideas about what they need on to them. If you ask them, for example, if they need to see a vet, it might be a foreign idea to them as they haven't separated from Nature's way of healing as we have.

Animals separate from their bodies much easier than we do when it comes time to die. Sometimes an animal companion will sacrifice himself in order to promote healing for his human companion. In this case, encourage the human to open and receive the gift of healing or growth that the animal offered. Some disease symptoms of animals are messages for the human, in which case you should convey those to the human, then communicate to the animal that it no longer needs to hold those symptoms. For your own animal companions convey to them that they don't need to communicate to you by getting ill or dying accidentally. If it is their time to die, use Raku to separate your energy fields with theirs, bless them and thank them for all their gifts. After they pass, you can connect to their spirit in "heaven."

Animals love when you keep your Primary Energies connected to your symbol. The psychic energy tends to go toward whatever you are intensely staring or looking at. This will make an animal move away from you. Check that you stay connected to your symbol and soften or relax your eyes.

- **Horses connect you to your spirituality.** Reiki will accelerate all healing of wounds. Work systematically from body to tail or wherever you are drawn to go. If a horse is in shock, panic or is wild, beam Reiki from a distance. Watch for indicators such as sighing, licking of lips, shifting body from one hip to another that they are responding to the Reiki. If they have a block in energy flow, Reiki can create discomfort in that area before the excess energy releases. They may pull away or get agitated. Lessen the intensity by taking your hands off the area and beam Reiki from a distance instead. If they need to heal from a trauma, use Hon Sha to travel back to when the trauma happened (such as with a vet or farrier) and do Reiki healing at that time. Horses love Dai Ko Myo.

- **Dogs connect you to your heart:** Usually dogs just lay down as soon as you start to work on them like a limp dish rag. Reiki will help them heal, and clarify what's going on so that vets can make better diagnoses for them. Muscle test to enhance animal communication with dogs. They love Sei He Ki for everything!
- **Cats connect you to your mind:** They are highly telepathic and would prefer to just "beam" you their thoughts. They might be scornful of your muscle testing! They also love Reiki but they won't necessarily let you know it. Yes, they purr when they are happy, but they are also known to bite or grab you with their claws. Stop sending Reiki immediately if they are doing that. Cats are prone to bladder infections and then start peeing in areas beside their litter boxes. Use a reversed Cho Ku Rei to break down urine crystals in the bladder. In the peed areas, use the lightning bolt Raku to stop the cat from using that area. Cats, of course, love Hon Sha.

In Conclusion

What a remarkable journey you have been on! Don't be afraid to try out these different techniques. Reiki will never harm another.

Have fun with your Reiki healing adventures. Practice, practice, and practice some more! Check the Appendix for Advanced Reiki Training. Contact me if you have questions.

You are an amazing Old Soul helping the world shift into the New Earth energies!

Continue Your Healing Journey

Advanced New Earth Reiki Training

Learn advanced techniques, receive more energy meditations and get videos to all the chapters. ANERT includes techniques such as:

- Clearing and Healing the Bones or Blood
- Clearing Negative Guides (and inviting in new ones)
- Releasing Karmic Contracts and Vows
- New Reiki Sessions such as The Spiral and The Labyrinth Chakra Healing
- Soul-Body Fusion
- Healing The Emotional Body
- Transitioning Teenager's into Their Own Spiritual Alignment
- Healing and Clearing the Eyes
- Working with Color
- Healing the Mitochondria
- Working with the Energy or Ka Body

Additional Energy Meditations for you are:

- Going into the Void (Healing Depression)
- Tree Meditation for Clearing and Healing the Hara Line

To enroll and more information go to:

Crystalline Consciousness Technique and New Earth Reiki

Want to further your profession in the healing arts and create more powerful Reiki sessions? Take *Discovering the Map of Transformation* (CCT Professional Levels 1 and 2) and learn how to combine the CCT protocol with Reiki. Besides the CCT protocol you'll learn and receive:

- 3 New Activations
- How to do a CCT Reiki session

- Transformation Patterns and how they affect how people heal
- The I AM Meditation for soul level healing
- Group Circle Soul Chart that works with groups

For more information about upcoming classes, please contact gia at ramblerg@mac.com.

Expressing Your Purpose

This Crystalline Consciousness Technique class provides a fast and easy protocol to help you identify your purpose and express it in accelerated ways through your creative energy. It also helps with empathic overwhelm or sensitivity. Offered in 3 self-paced modules you'll learn and receive:

- The challenges of your creative energy and purpose and how to shift them
- Discovering Your Purpose meditation that takes you on an unforgettable journey
- Activation
- Protocol and how to apply it

To enroll and receive immediate access to the modules go here. If the link doesn't work, please copy and paste this url: scienceofenergyhealing.com/expressing-your-purpose

Glossary

Attunement–opening and connecting the energy fields, bodies, and channels to the Reiki field of energy. Activates the Reiki symbols in the hands for healing. Attunements are healing for the receiver.

Alchemical Point–when the body reaches a certain, critical vibrational point it sets off a spontaneous reorganization throughout the entire system bringing in greater coherency and higher vibration. This is a desired result in healing session.

Chakras–energy vortexes that organize energy as it enters the body. There are seven main ones used in Reiki sessions and two additional ones that are used in Empowered Reiki attunements.

Consciousness–energy of awareness and intelligence. There are many types of consciousness that make up the universe.

Core Energy/Essence–that energy that relates to our essential Selves or the Soul. Physically it is a column of light seated in the spine and connecting the chakras or energy vortexes in the central body. Optimally it radiates out through our entire energy field. When we work with someone, we want to connect core essence to core essence.

Energy Body–the consciousness in charge of regeneration and repair of our body and energy anatomy. When working with people we give information to the Energy Body, not only through our own intuitive awareness, but also from our own energy fields. The Energy Body interfaces between the conscious and the unconscious mind.

Energy Channels–includes the meridians, grounding cord and hara line. These channels exist for energy to circulate through the body as well as ground our physical and emotional bodies to the Earth.

Energy Field–the electromagnetic field that is created by the body and sits 3-5 feet around us. It is a protection element for our body systems.

Energy Healing–working with the organizing forces that create and infuse matter.

Enlightenment–literally the ability of the body to hold more light photons through all levels and systems, including the cells and DNA. This causes a greater electrical charge giving us a greater power on the planet. It also increases our understanding of how the universe works as light holds holographic information. Our free will determines how we use this power.

Free Will and Choice–our Souls have free will and choice on this planet. This spiritual attribute requires developing discernment and right use of power. As healers, we need to honor another person's free will and choice, if it seems contrary to our intuition.

Healing–refers to invoking unified states of order, alignment, integration and balance within our entire system. Creating synchronous relationships within the whole-being.

Horizontal Energies–those energies that connect us to our past and future as well as those we are in relationship with in this physical realm. In the Old Energy paradigms many of us were blocked vertically and only had horizontal connection. We are now in the times when we can have balanced vertical/horizontal energies enabling us to be more fully present in our bodies, if we so choose.

Immune System Response–when the entire immune system goes into fight or flight or throws up a mucous shield because of an unknown or misunderstood incoming light energy or spiritual expansion throughout the entire being. Some people are unable to turn off the fight or flight mechanism, until they experience adrenal exhaustion. Colds are about throwing up mucous shields so that incoming energies can't enter the energy fields. A person who is constantly experiencing an immune system response is asking for a switch from the immune system to the endocrine system as primary warning system for the body.

Indicator Signal—a body response either within ourselves or from the person we are working with that indicates when it is appropriate to move in a healing session. Common indicator signals are a change in energy felt in the hands, sighing, or just a "knowing."

Karma—unfinished lessons. Because we can hold a greater vibrational charge throughout our physical bodies at this time on the planet we can heal and release a vast majority of our Earth karma. This in turn increases our vibrational frequency. Each time we increase our vibration as we spiritually expand we access new levels of karma incurred when we last held the same vibration.

Personality Energy Grid—along with the physical body this is part of the housing, or protection, for the Soul. It includes the personality, psyche and ego, which are created from the soul's blueprint for the lessons and tasks it's learning each lifetime. The personality has developmental stages that help it hold more of a spiritual (electrical) charge as a person grows older. The personality and Soul can get out-of-sync from unresolved traumas or from unbalanced spiritual growth.

Quality of Presence—a person who has a highly coherent, vibrational energy field throughout his/her entire energetic anatomy. The greater quality of presence we carry as healers, the greater the results are for the receivers.

Vertical Energies—includes the physical body grounding cord, the emotional body's hara line, certain mental body energy grids around the head, Core energy, and the heavenly cords of light that extend upward through our whole spiritual body. All of our emotional needs are answered vertically. In the past many of us developed strong vertical energies but weren't able to express horizontally. This would build up tremendous frustration through the energy anatomy as the forward movement or growth of the Soul was affected.

The Words of Crystalline Consciousness Technique

We use these words vibrationally to set up fields in the New Earth energies.

- **Opening**: Refers to Phase One of the CCT protocol when the body hooks up to higher levels of consciousness.
- **Healing Chambers**: Refers to Phase Two of the CCT protocol which uses sacred geometry that is charged with specific life force frequencies. When setting up a crystalline energy field they are placed in the appropriate order for the day or for a healing session.
- **Intention**: Any spoken intent has high vibration because it is consciously chosen. When setting up your fields you have one intention which is: to stay protected and connected in harmony in the New Earth Energies.
- **Mastery**: Refers to Phase Three of the protocol which is a completion phase.

23 Crystal Vibrations

Appreciation—sensitive awareness; grateful.

Balance—stability; harmony of various elements.

Clarity—a quality of transparency or pureness.

Connection—the ability to relate.

Creativity—the ability to bring into form.

Empathy—ability to relate to another's feelings.

Empowerment—a state of power or authority.

Enthusiasm—a form of passion.

Expression—a showing of feeling; to voice in language.

Gratitude—thankfulness.

Growth—to expand in consciousness and form.

Harmony—a combination of parts into an orderly whole.

Leadership—the ability to guide or show the way.

Mastery—the integration of spiritual wisdom and biological development.

Openness—a state of accessibility. The mental state of allowing, without resistance.

Protection—to be shielded from injury, danger or loss.

Self-Responsibility—fully owning one's emotional, mental and energetic responses

Serenity—a state of peacefulness, calmness or tranquility.

Service—being of assistance to others; sharing your Purpose.

Stillpoint—the temporary cessation of rhythms in the body/mind leading to greater order and organization throughout all systems.

Support—being held in an energetic container of emotional, mental, and physical love

Synchrony—the result of being in right timing.

Trust—a confidence in the honesty, integrity, reliability, and justice of another person or the Universe.

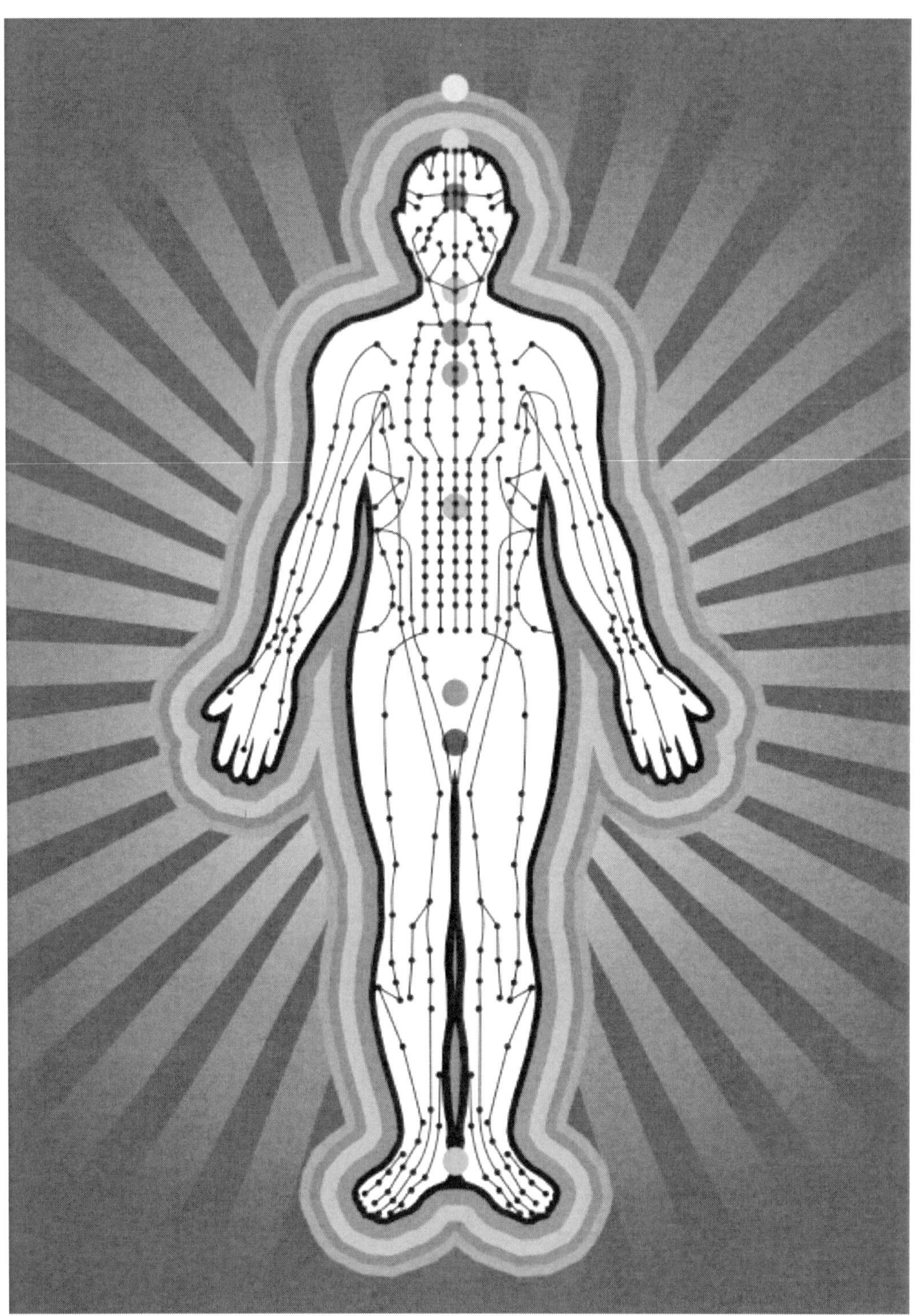

Type	Description	Characteristics
Energy Body	Field of energy that when seated in the body allows us to read	Has consciousness and innate body wisdom; Interfaces with the healing mechanisms of the body; Responds to intention and thought; Understands what order and timing for healing.
Energy Field	Extends beyond edge of body by 3 to 5 feet. Created by energy of Soul and life force from Nature. Optimally should be seated through the spine then extend out.	Protects the body systems from electromagnetic fields and aids in reading the immediate environment.
Subtle Bodies	Physical, Emotional, Mental, Spiritual energetic bodies that are different vibrational frequencies or octaves.	Each subtle body holds all others. Important that there is free flow of energy between all levels for healing and wholeness. Trauma may happen in one level then move into another.
Chakras	Seven energy centers vortexes located in the body. Names: Root or base; Sexual/Creative; Solar Plexus; Heart; Throat; 3rd Eye; Crown Crystalline Energy Centers: Head, Heart, Waist, Solar Plexus and Low belly, Feet	Organize energy as it enters the body. Have personal and spiritual developmental tasks. Each has color, organs, emotions. Can get congested where they overlap each other. Traditional Reiki sessions work with the chakras. Work with the CE System
Energy Streams	Information bands that influence us on many levels. Ancestral, cultural, racial, social, past, present and future are all different types of energy streams. Also called energetic genetics.	Influence how we think, act and ultimately heal. Distorted energetic patterns held within the energy streams can be cleared with Reiki and Intention.
Energy Channels	Meridians Microcosmic Orbit Grounding Cord Hara Line	Energy channels associated with the organs Used in Reiki Attunements to transfer energy into the body Anchors the physical body to the magnetic fields of the planet Anchors the emotional body to the magnetic fields of the planet

All Reiki Symbols

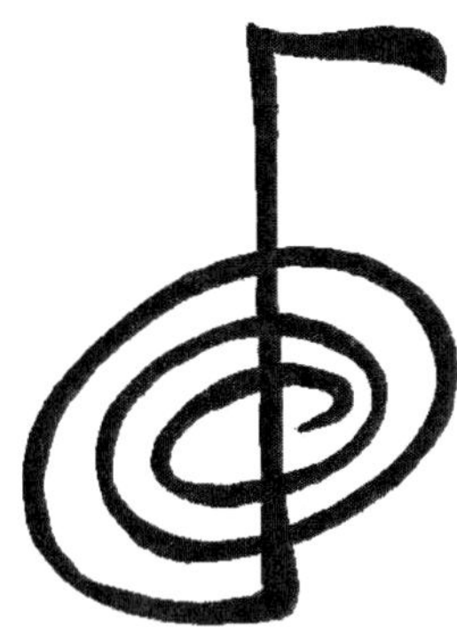

Cho-Ku-Rei

Sei-He-Ki

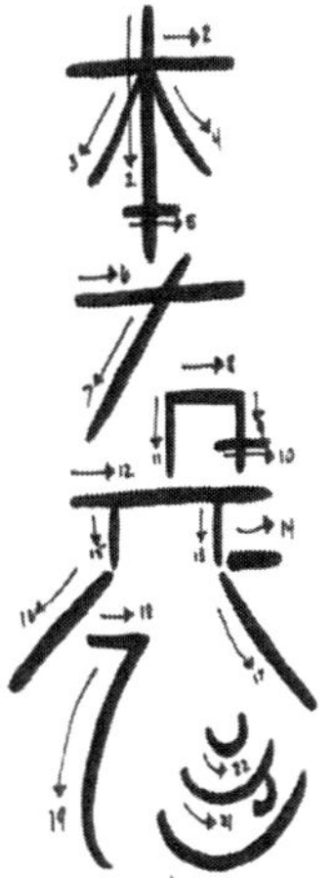

Hon-Sha-Ze-Sho-Nen

Dai-Ko-Myo

Ra-Ku

Fire Serpent

Protocol for Setting Up Crystalline Energy Fields

Step 1: Connect to your New Earth Reiki Symbol with your 3 primary energies. You can visualize this or state it.

Step 2: State your intention to stay protected and connected in harmony in the New Earth Energies.

Step 3: Define who's in your group (family, business, receiver of healing sessions, etc). Then state silently or out loud:

- "I ask to place the vibration of Opening in my individual crystalline energy field and my crystalline group field.
- I ask to place the Healing Chambers in my individual crystalline energy field and my crystalline group field in the appropriate order for my day (or this healing session).
- I ask to place the vibration of my Intention in my individual crystalline energy field and my crystalline group field.
- I ask to place the vibration of the 23 crystal vibrations in my individual crystalline energy field and my crystalline group field.
- I ask to place the vibration of Mastery in my individual crystalline energy field and my crystalline group field.
- I ask to connect to the Crystalline Grids of the Planet.
- I ask to connect to the Crystalline Energy Field."

For Reiki Master/Teachers

At this time there is no training to become a New Earth Reiki Teacher. To do so would take becoming a CCT Certified Teacher, first. However, if you are already a Reiki Master/Teacher from a traditional Usui training, you can use this manual as your workbook, and use the recorded attunements and activations that come with the manual. How to Set Up Fields would be taught through a recorded class. You will be able to teach the Reiki symbols and how to use them to your students as you would normally. For more information about buying wholesale copies of New Earth Reiki, please contact gia at ramblerg@mac.com.

For CCT Practitioners

If you are a trained CCT practitioner, you can add New Earth Reiki easily to your healing sessions. Please contact gia at ramblerg@mac.com for a special class in how to do this.

History of Usui Reiki

The history of Reiki is steeped in legend and myth. Because Reiki in the West was primarily a secret, oral tradition, many discrepancies arose between Reiki Masters. One version of the origin of Usui Reiki states that in the mid-1800s Mikao Usui, a Japanese Buddhist monk, began studying the ancient Sanskrit texts devised some 2500 years ago in India. He focused on the ancient symbols that were used to act as visual as well as sound mantras for the five levels on the Path of Enlightenment. Usui's interest was in the healing benefits that were gained with the use of the symbols. Traditionally this ancient knowledge was passed down orally from teacher to student and initiations were devised that opened or activated students to each new level. Usui had no such teacher to provide his initiation. Instead he went to the sacred Mt. Koriyama in Japan and entered a three-week period of meditation, fasting and prayer. On his last day, Usui saw a projectile of light coming toward him. At first he wished to run from it, for its power seemed too great for him to be able to contain, but he decided to accept what was coming even if it resulted in death. The light struck his third eye and he saw millions of rainbow bubbles as well as each of the Reiki symbols. He was given the information about each of them to activate healing energy.

According to the legend, when Usui descended Mt. Koriyama after his fast, he experienced four miracles. First, he painfully stubbed his toe. As he placed his hands on his foot they became red hot and the torn toe was healed. Later he ate a full meal, not wise after fasting for 21 days, and yet did not become sick. The woman who served his meal was suffering from a toothache and he healed her by placing his hands alongside her face. Finally, when Usui returned to his monastery, the director was in bed with an arthritis attack and he healed the monk.

Usui began working in the slums of Kyoto with the beggars. When he physically healed them he asked them to begin a new life. Instead many of them become angry about having their afflictions removed as their diseases provided their livelihoods. According to the legends this established in Usui's mind the need for some sort of energy exchange for true healing to occur on all levels. Although the energy exchange has been interpreted to mean an exchange of money, there are other ways to create an exchange of energy.

Usui and his follower, Hayashi, developed a clinic in which to treat people. Usui later died in 1930 and Hayashi, a retired Naval officer, died in 1941. Shortly before World War II broke out a Hawaiian woman, Hawayo Takata, who had trained under Hayashi, declared that she was his successor, appointed by Hayashi when war became imminent. Since Japan became cut off from the Western world there was no one to refute this statement. Takata developed many of the traditions surrounding Reiki in the Western world such as oral teachings, the secrecy of the symbols, the prohibitive cost of Reiki III ($10,000) as well as a long duration of apprenticeship.

When Takata died in 1980, she left no appointed successor. Phyllis Furomoto, Takata's daughter, appointed herself Grand Master causing conflict in the Reiki community. Gradually during the 80s many of the Reiki traditions, as created by Takata, came under question in the United States, including the high pricing of Reiki. Modern Usui Reiki has evolved from these concerns making it much more accessible to many people. Legends surrounding Mikao Usui, the attunement processes, the secrecy of the symbols, the strict oral tradition and the duration and cost of classes have all been challenged. Reiki, which was thought to be lost in Japan during World War II, is still practiced there today and evolved very differently from Western methods including records of a written manual by Master Usui.

Perhaps one of the greatest mysteries and delights of Reiki is that in spite of these differences, the power of Reiki is accessible to all who are attuned. The decades of oral tradition and secrecy around the symbols led to variations in the symbols, attunement processes, and different energy techniques taught with Reiki classes. Ultimately, none are wrong. There are only some more powerful than others. The spiritual power that a Reiki Master is able to hold and contain is what determines how powerful an attunement or healing session will be. With New Earth Reiki, the new energy system available to all on the planet holds tremendous amounts of power and light that enhances your Reiki healing powers.

Further Reading

Transformation: The Emergence of the Crystalline System by gia combs-ramirez

The Way of Transformation: Discovering the Divine Map to Unlock Your Highest Potential by gia combs-ramirez

Essential Reiki by Diane Stein

Essential Energy Balancing by Diane Stein

Reiki for A New Millennium by William Lee Rand

The Spirit of Reiki by Walter Lubeck, Frank Arjava Petter, and William Lee Rand

Japanese Reiki Techniques Video by Arjava Petter and Chetna Kobayashi

Reiki News Magazine at major book stores or www.reiki.org.

For more information on Crystalline Consciousness Technique™, please check the website ccthealing.com.

About The Author

gia combs-ramirez is the founder of Crystalline Consciousness Technique™ and New Earth Reiki. She is a transformative healer, coach and teacher with a worldwide practice. She began her conscious journey of transformation in 1989, learning bodywork at the New Mexico Academy of Healing Arts. Fascinated with the metaphysics of consciousness studies, transformation, soul purpose and energy healing, she continued her studies with shamanism, Reiki, EMF Balancing Technique®, Craniosacral Therapy, Oneness Blessing, the Akashic Records, and the metaphysics of personal and spiritual growth. In 2004, a new energy modality Crystalline Consciousness Technique™ downloaded into her awareness during a meditation. Through this modality, she's been studying Transformation at individual and global levels ever since. gia holds a Masters in Metaphysics from American Institute of Holistic Theology.

Made in United States
North Haven, CT
09 August 2022

22505226R00057